1972

TWELVE GREAT
AMERICAN NOVELS

Twelve Great American Novels

Arthur Mizener

THE BODLEY HEAD
LONDON SYDNEY
TORONTO

© Arthur Mizener 1967
SBN 370 00448   5
Printed in Great Britain for
The Bodley Head Ltd
9 Bow Street, London WC2
by Lowe and Brydone (Printers) Ltd., London
First published in Great Britain 1968

For

Robert Gutwillig

Contents

Preface

This book is intended to be practical, useful in a way that experience in teaching the novel suggests may be more needed than we sometimes recognize. Any close contact with people who are trying to read novels seriously, even able students who have had some experience of literature, suggests that readers are very uncertain of how to attack a novel. They are not sure they know what to look for and have little confidence in their ability to discover in any given novel what implications are important and, taken together, make its point. Much of the time they either frankly admit they do not see any point, or, in a kind of desperation, resort to some narrow and probably irrelevant critical doctrine about how novels should be written and to a set of moral and social judgments about the characters that mislead them.

How often readers are bored by Hawthorne because they find his novels static and posed—as indeed they are—when they have some-how got the notion that fluent action and a lively, informal style are essential to a good novel; how often they condemn Cooper because his novels have none of the minute analysis of feelings that they have somehow learned to think is the only virtue a novel can have. How often they confidently affirm that Faulkner is a bad novelist because

his characters are nasty people who think all the time about incest—
or that Henry James is because his characters are not. In these circumstances it may be useful to take a selection of the great novels of
American literature and try to start readers off with them. This, then,
is a book for the reader who wants help in reading these novels for
himself—not for the unintelligent reader, but for the interested one
who does not feel entirely at home with novels when he tries to read
them seriously.

The novels I have discussed make up a very small proportion of
the good novels in American literary history. We have only to remind
ourselves of the many other good novels written by even the few
writers dealt with here to see that. Nor ought readers to suppose that
what is said here is all that can profitably be said about these books.
There is neither thorough coverage of the history of American fiction
nor thorough critical treatment of any single novel here. Even if I
were capable of these things, I am not at all sure they would be useful
to the kind of reader I have in mind. The intelligent curious reader
wants to carry on on his own, once he has seen a direction that looks
as if it might be interesting to go in. All I have tried to do is to suggest to him—without producing an exhaustive list of examples—the
various kinds of novels that exist in American fiction, and to say only
enough about a famous example of each kind to indicate the way it
has to be read if its value is to be fully appreciated.

The discussions of the twelve works dealt with exist for themselves;
they have not been written with half an eye on some thesis that this
book is trying to prove. It has no thesis. These discussions are, however, held together by a general idea that is a commonplace among
critics and is, I believe, perfectly sound as far as it goes, though it
does not account for everything in the novels discussed (no generalization does). I hope this too may be useful; certainly it is confusing
and discouraging to readers if they are asked to contemplate what
may seem to them an almost endless variety of novels, each unique
in itself and therefore a new problem, without some sense that the
variety is not endless and that an order—preferably one that has

some relation to the culture that produced these works—can be detected beneath the confusion.

The desire to be useful to such readers has also led me to avoid, as far as I am able to, all novelties of interpretation. My hope is that I have represented these novels as what the majority of experienced and sympathetic readers agree they are; my ambition is to make it possible for the unpracticed reader to see them that way; it is not to provide him with "interestingly" eccentric and surprising conceptions of them. For this reason, too, I have tried to avoid minute analyses of the kind professional critics entertain one another with.

My idea has rather been to suggest for each novel the kind of mind that the reader confronts, to show the way the novel as a whole represents that mind in both what it expresses and in the way it does so, and to look closely at just enough passages to make the reader feel what is one of the greatest excitements of novel reading: the almost miraculous way in which a great writer's sense of things flows with perfect consistency into the innumerable details of his fiction until we almost feel—at least for the moment in which we apprehend it as it really is and are enthralled by it—that the problem of the one and the many has been solved; or, as Coleridge put it in his grand way when he was defining a poem, that we are in the presence of a composition which "is discriminated by proposing to itself such delights from the whole as is compatible with a distinct gratification from each component part."

Dr. Johnson once said that "he rejoiced to concur with the common reader" in his admiration for Gray's "Elegy." It is not an easy attitude to take without sounding condescending, and not many critics in our time appear interested even to try. Yet it is difficult to understand how anyone can have been a teacher without recognizing how necessary it is to try, how much the intelligent untrained reader—what Dr. Johnson meant by "the common reader"—needs that concurrence, and how futile and finicking in its overspecialized way the critic's own work becomes if he fails to achieve it. The humanistic discipline that has lost its desire to concur with the common reader ceases to be human.

Introduction

A useful way of looking at American novelists is to notice that they have always tended to divide into two groups according to what seemed to them the significant aspect of the reality men confront. This choice affects the fundamental purpose of fiction, the very conception of reality itself embodied in a novel, and thus largely determines the writer's conception of events and of characters and of the relations between them, as well as the way he will use the novel's resources of expression.

Men's conceptions of what aspect of reality is significant are always to some extent divided between objective and subjective reality, between "outer" and "inner" reality. "Thus is man," as Sir Thomas Browne said, "that great and true Amphibium whose nature is disposed to live . . . in divided and distinguished worlds." He is faced, on the one hand, by an outer reality that seems to be largely beyond his control and yet extremely important in determining what he thinks and does—the automatic processes of his own body, the uncontrollable forces of the physical world and of the social institutions that surround his self and press upon it constantly. On the other hand, there is the inner reality of that self, the fluent, kaleidoscopic drift of the affective life that is the foundation of consciousness. This affective life seems to exist, to an important extent, independent of his perception of outer reality and its influences on him and, at least partly, to determine that perception and to be prior to any reasoning about it.

These two realities clash in men's consciousnesses in thousands of ways. Apparently it is possible for them to accept—at least consciously—the authority of one of them and to deny the significance of the other, but Thoreau's famous assertion that most men lead lives of quiet desperation suggests that most men do not—or at least that most Americans do not. There are no doubt interesting historical—social and political—explanations for their not doing so; we ought to consider them, but we must always remember that in doing so we are cutting the Gordian knot—assuming, that is, that outer reality, the reality history deals with, is the significant one and that inner reality is to be explained in terms of it. Such explanations will not convince men who are committed to the inner reality. They will say —as did Tennyson when he was confronted by the implications of Darwin's theory—that "the heart stands up and cries, 'I feel,' " that these explanations are not significantly true. In any event, what concerns us most here is not primarily the nature of this conflict in man's consciousness but its consequences for the novel, and particularly its consequences for the novel in America, where, for whatever reasons, the conflict between these two realities has been specially exacerbated.

An habitual reliance on one or the other of these two realities produces a clearly recognizable kind of fiction. The novelists for whom outer reality is the significant one are concerned to make clear the true nature of outer reality, to show its modes of operation, and to trace its effects on men. For them the significant life of men is the way men reflect in their conduct the consequences of these forces; it consists in their relation to their physical and social surroundings and in the ways their conscious thoughts and attitudes are shaped by them. For such novelists what a man *does*—and his conscious reasons for doing it—are the important things. They write novels of action in which the plots illustrate conflicts between men or between men and nature that are socially and politically significant, and what concerns them about their characters is what illustrates and emphasizes this significance.

These characters meditate and moralize to themselves about what happens to them, but they are not given interior monologues that present the movements of their consciousnesses directly and for their own sakes. Their meditations are used to indicate the effects on them of the exterior world, and novelists of this kind, particularly in the nineteenth century, often reinforce these meditations with disquisitions of their own. As a consequence, the eloquent moments in their novels tend to be moments of rhetoric, as they are in Cooper and Dos Passos, or of vivid reasoning, as they are in Cozzens, rather than moments of lyric outcry, as they are in Melville, or of intense spiritual irony, as they are in Hawthorne. In Cooper and Dos Passos especially, the characters are interesting as types rather than as individuals and are of almost no psychological interest at all. There is nothing subtle about Natty Bumpo or Charley Anderson, but as we watch them we are acutely aware that large ranges of significant public experience are summed up by their lives. The great moments in such novels are moments of external difficulty or of violence in which the moral superiority of the right social or political attitude is brought home to the reader.

The novelist for whom inner reality is the significant one is concerned above all with the movement of mood and feeling, either within himself or within his characters. Reality is the inner world of consciousness itself, not the outer world of events. The most fully developed form for the presentation of this reality is the symbolic novel, the novel in which the events that constitute the plot exist primarily, not for themselves, but as symbols of the various feelings that constitute the author's consciousness. Frequently, especially in the nineteenth century, a novel of this kind has long sermons or "essays" that emphasize the symbolic meaning of the events, as Melville's *Moby Dick* has. If the novelist's sense of inner reality is organized according to some doctrine or dogma, as Hawthorne's partly was, this kind of novel tends toward allegory.

A slightly less extreme commitment to inner reality is represented by the kind of novel that presents events that are not symbolic in themselves, but shows them entirely through the eyes of a narrator whose consciousness is made so vivid that we are sure only of what the narrator thinks the events are and not at all of what, as we say, they really are. A similar effect is produced by a kind of novel very fashionable in the 1960's, the kind in which the external events the narrator lives through have an independent reality of their own, but in which we are so deeply involved in the account of the narrator's moods and feelings that runs parallel with his description of the events, that only these moods and feelings really matter to us. This is especially so when the feelings have no recognizable connection with the events or are in contrast with the responses these events ordinarily evoke, as, for example, in Norman Mailer's *American Dream*.

Another form often used by novelists concerned with inner reality is the one in which an objective narrative of events is interspersed with long passages of interior monologue representing the consciousnesses of the characters. This can be carried to the point where all, or nearly all, of the novel consists of such monologues, as does Faulkner's *The Sound and the Fury,* where only the last section is not an interior monologue. Finally, an author may present his entire story in the third person and yet do so in a style so charged with his personal feelings and his private conception of the story's meaning that we are as much aware of the life of his consciousness as we are of the existence of the events of his story. Something like this occurs in Fitzgerald's *Tender Is the Night,* where its effect is reinforced by our knowledge that the hero has a good deal in common with his author, and in many of Faulkner's third-person narrations.

We seldom feel that the plots of any of these kinds of novels have much meaning or that the events that occur in them matter for themselves. Nor do we feel that the characters sum up for us the representative experience of a time and place, even when the novels deal with historically important occasions, as in some sense *The Scarlet Letter* and *The Sound and the Fury* both do. But the life and the quality of a consciousness—the author's or the characters' or both—are there for us in all their subtlety and variety. We can trace their slightest movements and often catch them on the verge of some final metaphysical conclusion determined by the way they feel about their own feelings. This is certainly true of *Moby Dick,* so true that the novel is sometimes called a metaphysical romance, and of *The Scarlet Letter;* and it is true of Quentin Compson in *The Sound and the Fury* if not of Faulkner himself.

The differences between the two kinds of novels these two notions of significant reality lead men to produce are illustrated by the difference between the novels of the first two important writers in the history of the American novel, Cooper and Hawthorne, both of whom wrote during the second quarter of the nineteenth century.

B

JAMES FENIMORE COOPER
1789-1851

The Deerslayer

1841

Cooper was the first entirely American novelist to win an international reputation, and the extent of that reputation is indicated by the fact that he was widely known as "the American Sir Walter Scott," a comparison that flattered neither writer. Diplomatically friendly on the surface, Scott and Cooper never really liked one another. In ways typical of the societies of their native lands, Sir Walter observed of Cooper that he had "a good deal of the manner, or want of manner, of his countrymen," and Cooper thought Sir Walter hopelessly lacking in seriousness. It is difficult not to sympathize with Scott in this situation; Cooper was a maddeningly tactless man: his idea of how to ingratiate himself with the English was to announce loftily on his arrival in London that "the Thames [was] a stream of trivial expanse."

He was equally tactless at home, spending his later years in libel suits and in fruitless quarrels with his neighbors over his property rights in Cooperstown, the lovely upstate New York village his father had founded on Lake Otsego, the scene of *The Deerslayer*. With these neighbors, Cooper asserted his genuine if old-fashioned liberal individualism by insisting on his freedom to be the kind of man he chose to be, or what he perversely enjoyed calling his democratic right to be

1

a gentleman. It was not the sort of remark to warm the hearts of men who thought—as Cooper bitterly put it—that democracy consists in standing about on street corners together, spitting. He was a man crotchety in opinion, defensive about his own dignity, and almost as tactless as he was demanding of tact in others: "a gentleman," as D. H. Lawrence put it, "in the worst sense."

Nevertheless, nearly everything valuable in Cooper's work derives from the tension within him between his commitment to the democratic idea of individual excellence and his consciousness of democracy as the majority opinion of common men, however common. Cooper faced with heroic tactlessness a dilemma of American democracy that is often unobserved or ignored by conventional liberalism and has been clearly outlined in our own century only by the so-called Southern Agrarians—unfortunately at a time (the 1930's) when their argument was quickly buried under a midden of popular Marxism. But the dilemma they made clear is still a more or less concealed element in the social debate between the North and the South.

At the center of democratic theory there is a conflict between the belief that society must provide for every individual the maximum freedom and opportunity to develop his own intellectual and moral capacities, however far that development may carry him beyond the ideas and feelings of his fellows, and the belief that majority opinion has a sacred right to determine what ideas and feelings are right and an obligation to make sure all members of the community conform to them. Because of the ideological circumstances of the United States' origins, this conflict was particularly violent during the early days of its existence, and the difficulties it creates are at the heart of Cooper's novels.

Cooper's life was a sadly comic version—as his novels are a serious one—of this democratic paradox, so neatly defined by Thoreau when he said that whenever a man is righter than his neighbors there is already a majority of one. Like the Adams family in New England and Jefferson in the South, Cooper belonged to that minority of early Americans for whom the justification of their society was its opportunity for the achievement of excellence, not its insistence on the sacredness of majority opinion. As a political force this minority was quickly crushed between the commercialism of Alexander Hamilton and the populism of Andrew Jackson that still remain the two major attitudes of American politics, but the dilemma Cooper embodied in his novels remains.

The best of his novels make fables for this dilemma out of adventure stories that combine the universal Western myth of the Noble Savage with a direct knowledge of the American frontier. The last— in time of composition—and the greatest of Cooper's five novels about his mythological frontier hero, Natty Bumpo, is *The Deerslayer*. In it, Natty matures into the hero he will remain for the rest of his life. He and his closest friend, the heroic Delaware Indian Chingachgook, the Great Serpent, are on their first independent expedition. They are seeking to rescue the beloved of Chingachgook, the Indian maiden Hist-oh!-Hist, who has been abducted by a renegade Delaware and carried off to an enemy tribe, the Mingos.

The novel opens with Natty on his way to meet Chingachgook at Lake Glimmerglass, Cooper's name for Lake Otsego. He is traveling with a hunter named Hurry Harry, who is on his way to visit a beautiful and daring girl named Judith Hutter. Judith lives in a house set on a sandbar in the middle of Glimmerglass, with her father and her simple-minded sister, Hetty. Judith, it turns out, will not marry Hurry, but neither can she have Deerslayer, with whom she falls in love, because she has had a love affair with a British officer from the nearby fort and has thus offended sexually against the established moral code of the white man's culture. Deerslayer has an almost anthropological tolerance for the different moral attitudes—what he calls "the gifts"—of white and Indian cultures, but he is rigidly, even puritanically, insistent that the members of each culture be true to their own. So, at the end of the novel, Judith Hutter goes regretfully off to wicked old Europe as the mistress of the British officer who first seduced her. She is the first example of a character that will appear again and again in American literature, from Hester Prynne, the proud and passionate heroine of Hawthorne's *Scarlet Letter,* to Charlotte Stant, the brilliant adventuress of Henry James's *Golden Bowl.*

When Deerslayer and Hurry Harry reach Glimmerglass and make contact with Chingachgook, they find that the Mingos are already there and on the warpath, so they join forces with the Hutters for defense, and set out to rescue Hist-oh!-Hist. The resulting narrative is filled with brilliant action, but *The Deerslayer* cannot be read simply as an adventure story. Cooper makes every incident in it a dramatization of the moral attitudes embodied by his characters and does not hesitate to keep us standing about for long stretches, at the most exciting moments, while he or Deerslayer points up the moral of the action.

These sermons, like everything else in Cooper's novels, are written in an insensitive, mechanical version of the genteel style of the eighteenth century. Even at the most dramatic and emotional moments, Cooper does not deviate from this rather dry and pompous style, and —as do the styles of other writers of adventure stories of his time, like Scott and Horace Walpole—it often seems in almost absurd contrast with the subject. Thus his strong feeling for the natural beauty of Lake Otsego (Glimmerglass in the novel) provokes from him a sentence like the following, "The size of the lake brought all within the reach of human senses, while it displayed so much of the imposing scene at a single view, giving up, as it might be, at a glance, a sufficiency to produce the deepest impressions." The impetuous love felt by the passionate Judith Hutter for Deerslayer he describes by saying, "Judith . . . seemed to find pleasure in consulting and advising with her new acquaintance, whose indifference to danger, manly devotion to herself and her sister, guilelessness of manner, and truth of feeling had won rapidly on both her imagination and her affections." Not that this style is pointless; on the contrary, it is the logical if somewhat mechanical and insensitive expression of the conservative, rational individualist, the gentleman whom Cooper asserted with such passion it was his democratic right to become. But its orderly, dispassionate, reasonable tone is incongruous with the passionately romantic subject matter it is often required to express.

Written as they are in this style the sermons in *The Deerslayer* may seem to modern readers both awkward interruptions of the narrative and dull in themselves, but Cooper's instinct is right; it is the moral drama of his novels that gives them their power. They are myths for democratic culture, as puzzling in their ultimate public meaning, despite their surface obviousness, as any metaphysical romance is in its private meaning, despite its popular rhetorical charms.

Consider, for example, the great moment near the beginning of the novel when Deerslayer achieves his manhood by killing his first enemy in meticulously honorable combat. The scene opens with Deerslayer landing his canoe on a dangerous point of land on the shore of Lake Glimmerglass. " 'Twas a trying moment," says Cooper, "for any novice, nor was there the encouragement which even the timid sometimes feel, when conscious of being observed and commended. . . . Notwithstanding all these circumstances, the most experienced veteran in forest warfare could not have conducted himself better. Equally free from recklessness and hesitation, his advance was marked by a sort of philosophical prudence, that appeared to render him superior to all motives but those that are best calculated to effect his purpose. Such was the commencement in forest exploits, that afterwards rendered this man, in his way, . . . as renowned as many a hero whose name has adorned the pages of works more celebrated than legends simple as ours can ever become."

As Deerslayer's canoe glides toward the shore, he is fired on from the woods and instantly drops to the bottom of his canoe, as if wounded. "A yell—it came from a single voice—followed, and an Indian leaped from the bushes upon the open area of the point bounding toward the canoe. This was the moment the young man desired. He rose on the instant, and leveled his own rifle on his uncovered foe; but his finger hesitated about pulling the trigger on one whom he held at such a disadvantage. This little delay, probably, saved the life of the Indian, who bounded back into the cover as swiftly as he had broken out."

Deerslayer leaps from his canoe and also seeks cover in the woods, where he quickly detects the Indian reloading his rifle behind a tree.

"Nothing would have been easier," says Cooper, "than to spring forward, and decide the affair by a close assault on his unprepared foe; but every feeling of Deerslayer revolted at such a step, although his own life had just been attempted from a cover . . . instead of advancing to fire, he dropped his rifle to the usual position of a sportsman in readiness to catch his aim, and muttered to himself, unconscious that he was speaking,—'No, no—that may be red-skin warfare, but it's not a Christian's gifts. Let the miscreant charge, and then we'll take it out like men. . . . No, no; let him have time to reload, and God will take care of the right!' "

This is an exciting and dramatic scene, and it has all the immense fictional advantage of being concerned with a display of remarkable skill in a very dangerous situation. But the meaning it dramatizes is a social one. What Deerslayer represents are public values, what the best kind of Christian white man feels; we have no sense of any unique, private self he may possess. Natty Bumpo is here, as always, the representative man—or rather the representative hero—of a culture that blends the European qualities it brought with it to the West with the qualities the frontier (and in Natty's case, even long training among the Indians) has developed in its representatives.

When the Indian has reloaded, he quickly exposes himself, thinking Deerslayer is still on the point. "The Deerslayer stepped from behind his own cover, and hailed him. 'This-a-way, red-skin; this-a-way, if you're looking for me. . . . I'm young in war, but not so young as to stand on an open beach to be shot down like an owl, by daylight. It rests on yourself whether it's peace, or war, atween us; for my gifts are white gifts, and I'm not one of them that thinks it valiant to slay human mortals, singly, in the woods.' " The two parley and agree to separate in peace. Then, just as Deerslayer is stepping carelessly into his canoe, his quick eye tells him that the Indian is about to fire on him from the bushes. Aiming where he knows the savage's body must be from this glimpse of his head, Deerslayer fires from the hip just as the Indian fires and misses. The Indian comes charging out of the bushes, tomahawk in hand, but, as Cooper says, "Deerslayer moved

not, but stood with his unloaded rifle fallen against his shoulders."
Forty feet from Deerslayer, the Indian makes a feeble attempt to
throw his tomahawk and falls. "I know'd it—I know'd it!" Deerslayer
exclaims. ". . . say what you will, for or a'gin 'em, a red-skin is by
no means as sartain with powder and ball as a white man. Their gifts
don't seem to lie that-a-way."

Deerslayer then goes up to the dying Indian, takes his head on his
lap, and with all the sympathy of his tolerance for other creeds than
his own, when they are sincerely held, he endeavors to "sooth his
anguish" by preaching a little sermon, in the Indian's own terms,
about the happy hunting grounds. Then he painstakingly does what his
white gifts require of the representative hero and forgives the Indian.
"Now, as for myself," he says, "I overlook altogether your designs
a'gin my life; first, because no harm came of 'em; next, because its
your gifts, and natur', and trainin', and I ought not to have trusted
you at all; and finally and chiefly because I can bear no ill-will to a
dying man, whether heathen or Christian." At the moment of his
death, the Indian asks Deerslayer his name, and when he hears it,
shakes his head. "Eye sartain—finger lightning," he says. "Aim—
death, great warrior soon. No Deerslayer—Hawkeye—Hawkeye—
Hawkeye. Shake hand." Thus Deerslayer kills, for the first time, with
Christian honorableness, and earns his warrior's title, Hawkeye.

Every incident in *The Deerslayer* is similarly charged with large
public meanings. No sooner, for example, has Hurry Harry arrived
at Glimmerglass than he and old Hutter, sublimely confident of their
white superiority, have concocted an innocently brutal scheme for collecting Mingo scalps. When Deerslayer points out that scalping is
contrary to white gifts, Hurry Harry replies, unanswerably, that the
white man's government has offered a bounty for Indian scalps. The
two are, of course, captured by the Indians before they can do any
damage, and the simple-minded Hetty goes to the Mingo camp to
save them by reading the Indians passages from the Bible. The Indians will not touch her because she is not normal and according to
their "gifts" the abnormal are sacred, but when she has finished her

reading, they solemnly ask her how it is that Christians seek Indian scalps if they believe what she has been reading them.

In this way Cooper makes even his minor characters into lucid embodiments of powerful and typical moral attitudes and uses the exciting action of his story to dramatize the conflicts among these attitudes. Hurry Harry and old Hutter represent what Cooper thought was the characteristically self-assured and thoughtless brutality of the average white man; they show Cooper's conception of the democratic majority. Deerslayer is the rare exception among white men, the one who has taken full advantage of democratic society's precious opportunity for self-development to become the kind of being democracy ought to produce and indeed must if it is to justify its existence, the man whose skill in action is always a manifestation of a naturally cultivated superiority of moral insight and integrity.

Cooper is the first important writer of the tradition in American literature that leads through Mark Twain's novels of sensitive savages to those of Ernest Hemingway, who once said that all modern American literature comes from one book by Mark Twain called *Huckleberry Finn*. But it does not, for there is another way of meeting the dilemma of American experience, the way that is represented by the great writer of the philosophical romance, Nathaniel Hawthorne.

NATHANIEL HAWTHORNE
1804-1864

The Scarlet Letter

1850

Hawthorne was nearly a generation—fourteen years to be precise—younger than Cooper, a New Englander who lived much of his life in Concord, Massachusetts, where he was the friend of Emerson and Thoreau and a member of the transcendentalist group that was the heart of what is sometimes called the American renaissance. He was an intensely subjective, turned-in man; there was a period of his life, before his marriage, when he almost withdrew from the world completely, and even in later life Emerson said of him that, despite their closeness, they had never really talked. Henry James, Senior, his contemporary, once described Hawthorne at a dinner party of literary people in New York as looking like a "rogue who suddenly finds himself in a company of detectives." His novels are full of the imagery of mirrors and his scenes are always static, carefully composed, and often framed, in such a way as to emphasize their literal artificiality, the inwardness of their reality.

For Hawthorne, in short, reality was always profoundly subjective, whereas for Cooper, it was objective—social and political. All Hawthorne's novels are what he once called a group of his short stories, "allegories of the heart." He had the luck to live at one of those mo-

ments in history when a great explanation of the human heart—New
England Calvinism—though still powerful over men's minds, was beginning to decline, so that Hawthorne's allegories are of a heart torn
between a Puritan sense of the tragic evil of man's nature and a humane sympathy with man's natural passions. There was almost nothing he could not, in his way, understand about the human consciousness. "He had," as the greatest of his followers, Henry James, put it,
"a cat-like faculty of seeing in the dark"; he is the first great writer
of the tradition of psychological, subjective fiction in American literature that leads through Melville to Henry James and, ultimately, to
Faulkner—who has a good deal more in common with Hawthorne
than is evident at first glance.

Hawthorne's undoubted masterpiece is *The Scarlet Letter,* written
less than a decade after Cooper's *Deerslayer.* In form it is a nearly
perfect example of the static, pictorial design that Hawthorne's dream-
vision of the world demanded, given texture and solidity by the detailed representation of the Puritan-New England world of a hundred
years before the date of its writing that is the scene of the story.

In the first chapter of *The Scarlet Letter,* Hester Prynne, its heroine, is made to stand on the scaffold in the town's marketplace so
that the whole community may stare at the scarlet letter on her breast
that is the public sign of her adultery. From the time of this public
display of her guilt until the novel is almost completed, Hester lives
with proud dignity in a lonely cabin, earning a living for herself and
her illegitimate child, Pearl, by her skill as a seamstress—a skill she
uses, with symbolic significance, to make the sign of her adultery, the
scarlet letter she wears on her breast, a thing of dazzling sensuous
splendor, and to provide somber but rich clothing for the Puritan dig-
nitaries of the community. She is much too proud to be defiant, even
if her own mind were not, as it is, divided about her situation; but
there is much in all this to suggest that she has not entirely subdued
the passion of her heart or accepted as just the punishment the community has forced her to endure.

In Chapter Twelve—exactly halfway through the novel—her un-

exposed partner in sin, the town's leading clergyman, Arthur Dimmesdale, also stands on the scaffold on which Hester had been forced to
expose her scarlet letter to the whole community, but he does so at
night, alone, seeking vainly to expiate his own sin by exposing his
scarlet letter in the dark, to no one. After this effort, for the rest of
the novel, the torture of his unpurged conscience grows greater and
greater, making him, ironically, a more and more eloquent and successful preacher.

The linked lives of Hester Prynne and Arthur Dimmesdale are
brought to a common climax in the novel's next-to-last chapter, Chapter Twenty-Three. There Dimmesdale reaches the height of that eloquence that has been created by the pain of his concealed guilt and
achieves a great public triumph with his moving election sermon.
Then, shaken almost to the point of fainting by his own suffering, he
joins the procession of town worthies as they move through the town
from the church. When Dimmesdale reaches the scaffold in the center
of the town, he stops and calls to his side Hester Prynne and their
daughter. With "the little hand of the sin-born child clasped in his"
and with Hester supporting him, he climbs the scaffold and there confesses his guilt in broad daylight to the whole town. The he dies in
Hester's arms.

In order to experience the power of Hawthorne's novel, the reader
must subdue his habitual impulse to look for the interest of the novel
in the gradual progress and development of the plot. It is of course
true that *The Scarlet Letter* has a plot that arouses some interest:
Will Arthur Dimmesdale purge his conscience by public confession
and ruin his career, or will he fail to do so and be destroyed by his
own unconfessed guilt? There is even a moment when the novel suggests a third possibility, that Arthur and Hester may run away together and "start their lives over."

But the real interest of *The Scarlet Letter* does not lie in this plot,
as is clear from the way Hawthorne consistently fails to take advantage
of its opportunities for suspense and for the excitement of violent
action. He is interested in something other than the effects of plot, and

what that is, is indicated by the deliberately static and carefully balanced pictorial ordering of the narrative, with its equally spaced and carefully similar scenes on the scaffold. The narrative does not progress from one to the other of these scenes. Each confronts the hero or heroine with the same problem; in the first Hester is forced to make a public confession of her sin but remains defiant in her heart; in the second, Arthur Dimmesdale is humble in heart but incapable of making his confession of guilt public; in the third, he makes a voluntary and public confession of his guilt and accepts his responsibility for both Hester and their child. The interest and excitement of this representation lies in the deep and subtle perception of the spiritual life with which Hawthorne, by the management of the particulars of his story, surrounds these key scenes.

Just as the reader must, in order to see this in the novel, look at its form in the right way, so he must be careful not to be deceived by the somewhat formal diction and syntax of Hawthorne's style into overlooking the precision with which it expresses every turn of Hawthorne's complicated thoughts and feelings about the spiritual life that is represented by his story. To the casual eye, Hawthorne's style may appear to differ little from Cooper's, and it does in fact belong to the same general tradition of prose, the slightly elevated style of the educated man of the early nineteenth century. The reader who turns from Cooper to Hawthorne will see the general resemblance at once in a sentence like, "There dwelt, there trod the feet of one with whom she deemed herself connected in a union, that, unrecognized on earth, would bring them together before the bar of final judgment, and make that their marriage-altar, for a joint futurity of endless retribution." But, seen in their contexts, even sentences like this one are not the mechanical collections of slightly hollow conventional phrases Cooper's sentences generally are. In Hawthorne's hands this style becomes an expressive device of great delicacy and power, as it never does in Cooper's. The reader can see how well it works at its best by watching how easily and unobtrusively Hawthorne uses it to make the small details of each scene meaningful parts of the spiritual drama within his own consciousness, which is the real point of his novel.

The novel begins, for example, by placing the reader, like a fixed camera, in the middle of the crowd that is waiting for Hester—her prison sentence for adultery now served—to emerge from the town jail. "Like all that pertains to crime"—says Hawthorne, speaking, we notice, not just of the *punishment* of crime but of *all* that pertains to it—"[this jail] seemed never to have known a youthful era. Before this ugly edifice, and between it and the wheel-track of the street, was a grass-plot, much overgrown with burdock, pig-weed, apple-peru, and such unsightly vegetation, which evidently found something congenial in the soil that had so early borne the black flower of civilized society, a prison." This is an almost perfect example of the way Hawthorne's imagination works. It starts with a literal description of natural vegetation, and then, halfway through the second sentence, it takes off into Hawthorne's peculiar kind of moral symbolism with the suggestion that the morally tainted soil that nourishes "the black flower of civilized society, a prison," is "evidently" "congenial" with this unsightly natural vegetation.

The passage goes on to an even more brilliant interweaving of natural description and moral symbolism. "But on one side of the portal, and rooted almost at the threshold, was a wild rose-bush, covered, in this month of June, with its delicate gems, which might be imagined to offer their fragrance and fragile beauty to the prisoner as he went in, and to the condemned criminal as he came forth to his doom, in token that the deep heart of Nature could pity and be kind to him"—even, Hawthorne seems to imply, if the shallow heart of man and, perhaps, the unrelenting heart of God, could not. He then adds that "there is fair authority for believing [this rose-bush] had sprung up under the footsteps of Anne Hutchinson, as she entered the prison-door."

Anne Hutchinson had been imprisoned and then driven into exile by the first synod of the Presbyterian Church and died at the hands of the Indians. Her crime had been to resist the public moral rigidity of the Puritan community. "Finding [this rose-bush]," Hawthorne concludes, "directly on the threshold of our narrative, that is about to issue from that inauspicious portal, we could hardly do otherwise than pluck one of its flowers, and present it to the reader. It may serve, let us hope, to symbolize some sweet moral blossom, that may be found along the track, or relieve the darkening close of a tale of human frailty and sorrow."

Out of that "inauspicious portal" with burdock and rose-bush on either side steps the adulteress Hester Prynne with her child in her arms. "On the threshold of the prison," says Hawthorne, "she repelled [the beadle], by an action marked with natural dignity and force of character, and stepped into the open air, as if by her own free will." "*As if* by her own free will"; the phrase concentrates all Hawthorne's Puritan doubts of the freedom of the human will and all his humanistic sympathy with those who acted on a belief in it. As Hester steps forth from this Puritan prison in the splendor of her dark beauty and the pride of her self-assertion, the crowd is astonished to see that the symbol of her shame, the letter A on her breast, is "of fine red cloth surrounded with an elaborate embroidery and fantastic flourishes of gold thread. . . . It was so artistically done, and with so much fertility and gorgeous luxuriance of fancy, that it had all the effect of a last and fitting decoration to the apparel which she wore." Fitting it certainly is in the proud and touching wrongness of its assertion of the luxuriance of the human fancy. A moment later, as Hester stands on the scaffold with Pearl in her arms, Hawthorne carries this irony to its climax.

Had there been a Papist among the crowd of Puritans, [he observes] he might have seen in this beautiful woman, so picturesque in her attire and mien, and with the infant at her bosom, an object to remind him of Divine Maternity, . . . something to remind him, indeed, by contrast, of the sacred image of sinless motherhood, whose infant was to redeem the world. Here, there was the taint of deepest sin in the most sacred quality of human life, working such effect, that the world was only the darker for this woman's beauty, and the more lost for the infant that she had borne.

Hester accepts her position in the Puritan community with proud humility; Hawthorne never suggests for a moment that it is possible for human beings to live alone, apart from the community. But neither does he allow Hester to deny her love for Arthur Dimmesdale, which is a silent defiance of the community: that love remains alive in her heart to the end. So for seven years she remains a proud, silent, awesome figure within the community where her sensitive and conscience-stricken seducer, Arthur Dimmesdale, lives his apparently—and, in most ways, genuinely—saintly life as an eloquent minister. Then it becomes evident that he is slowly dying of his hidden moral cancer.

His suffering is cunningly increased by a mysterious doctor named Roger Chillingworth, who turns out to be Hester's elderly, missing husband. Chillingworth's aim is to encourage Dimmesdale to continue his life of deception, knowing that it will give him his revenge by destroying Dimmesdale's soul as well as his body. His is the way of death, for himself as well as Dimmesdale: when Dimmesdale finally confesses, "old Roger Chillingworth knelt down beside him, with a blank, dull countenance, out of which the life seemed to have departed." The course Hester suggests to Dimmesdale is at least a way of life, the life of the passions; it may be a deception, but it is not a negation of all life. The course Dimmesdale finally chooses for himself kills him, but not until he has come alive again spiritually.

When Hester realizes that supporting the burden of his concealed guilt under the eyes of a community that thinks him almost a saint is slowly killing Dimmesdale, she arranges to meet him in the dark, powerful, pagan forest, far from the orderly Christian community of men, where "that wild, heathen Nature of the forest, never subjugated by human law, or illuminated by higher truth," as Hawthorne puts it, can add its influence to the appeal Hester means to make to Arthur. There—as Pearl, the unrestrainedly natural child of their too natural passion, plays about in the sunshine like some nymph—Hester urges

c

Arthur with all the loving energy of her passionate nature to escape
his intolerable life and begin again.

"Thou art crushed under this seven years' weight of misery,"
[she says to him.] "But thou shalt leave it all behind thee! It shall
not cumber thy steps, as thou treadest along the forest-path;
neither shalt thou freight the ship with it, if thou prefer to cross
the sea. Leave this wreck and ruin here where it hath happened.
Meddle no more with it! Begin all anew! Hast thou exhausted possibility in the failure of this one trial? Not so! The future is yet
full of trial and success. There is happiness to be enjoyed! There
is good to be done! Exchange this false life of thine for a true
one. . . . Preach! Write! Act! Do anything save lie down and
die! . . . Why shouldst thou tarry so much as one other day in
the torments that have so gnawed into thy life! . . . Up, and away!"

Dimmesdale, feeling for himself "the wild, free atmosphere of an
unredeemed, unchristianized, lawless region" and half carried away by
Hester's courageous commitment to the promises of man's natural
life, says wistfully,

"O Hester! thou tellest of running a race to a man whose knees
are tottering beneath him! I must die here! There is not the
strength or courage left me to venture into the wide, strange, dif-
ficult world, alone!" . . .
He repeated the word.
"Alone, Hester!"
"Thou shalt not go alone!" answered she, in a deep whisper.
Then, all was spoken!

It is a magnificent and moving moment, all the more so because,
after giving Hester the unanswerable question about the justice of
man's life (is it fair to give muddled men only one trial, as life does?),
Hawthorne has made us see how pitifully deluded she is, like some
Eve trying, after the fall, to persuade Adam that they can escape from
the inner reality, the spiritual consequences, of their own acts and find
another paradise, in which they can begin over again as if new-born.
We know that the torments that have gnawed into Arthur Dimmes-

dale's life have their cause within him, not outside, and that they will cumber his steps wherever he may go. It is marvelous, too, the way Hawthorne traces the movement of temptation within Arthur Dimmesdale as he responds to Hester's proposal. Trained casuist though he is, he forgets for a moment, in his anxiety to believe Hester, the inescapable fact of his own guilt and fixes unerringly on the difficulty she can tell him how to escape rather than on the one she cannot.

It is because he does not remain long deceived that Dimmesdale finally chooses to climb the scaffold and, with Hester and Pearl beside him, confess his guilt. "Is not this better," he asks Hester there, "than what we dreamed of in the forest?" But true to the death to her commitment Hester answers, "I know not! I know not! Better? Yea; so we may both die, and little Pearl die with us!" But old Roger Chillingworth, who had sought the death of Arthur Dimmesdale's soul, knows it is better. "Hadst thou sought the whole earth over," he says, as if he knew precisely what Hester had said to Arthur in the forest, "there was no place so secret—no high place nor lowly place, where thou couldst have escaped me—save on this very scaffold!"

Once, in the preface to a short story called "Rappaccini's Daughter," Hawthorne wrote an ironic commentary on himself as a writer. "His writings," he said, ". . . might have won him greater reputation but for an inveterate love of allegory, which is apt to invest his plots and characters with the aspect of scenery and people in the clouds, and to steal away the warmth of his conceptions . . . in any case, he generally contents himself with a very slight embroidery of outward manners,—the faintest possible counterfeit of real life,—and endeavors to create an interest by some less obvious peculiarity of the subject."

This is an ironic expression of an anxiety that will haunt American fiction throughout its history, its frustrated desire to satisfy a need for the vivid representation of objective reality, the outward world of people and manners, and at the same time to trace in detail the endless meanderings of what Hawthorne calls here "some less obvious peculiarity of the subject," that is, the multiple, mirrored activities of the inner consciousness. What Henry James, that most American of all novelists, called the "nutritive truth" of the history of American fiction is the intensity with which all American novelists feel both these realities, despite the temperamental inclination of each of them to emphasize one or the other, as Cooper emphasized objective reality and Hawthorne subjective.

HERMAN MELVILLE
1819-1891

Moby Dick

1851

Herman Melville was born in 1819, fifteen years after Hawthorne. He was brought up in comfortable circumstances. His father, a New York importer, came of a wealthy family that had been prominent in Boston since revolutionary days. His mother was descended from one of the notable New York Dutch families, the Gansevoorts. Her brother, the one member of the family on whom Melville could count in later days, was a banker in Albany—where Melville was sent to the Albany Academy for his secondary education—and a contemporary of Henry James's grandfather, also an Albany banker, who was busy accumulating the fortune on which the next two generations of the James family were to live.

But when Melville was thirteen, his father lost all his money and promptly died, and Melville, after trying his hand at being a bank clerk for a year or so, set out to roam the world as a seaman, jumping ship in Liverpool to live in its slums, and in the Marquesas to live with the savage Typees, serving on New England whalers and in the notoriously brutal American Navy, on one of whose ships, the frigate *United States,* he finally found his way back to Boston in 1844. With a good deal of social irony and perhaps even more intellectual seriousness, he called these years of roaming his "Harvard and Yale."

But his education did not, of course, cease with these bright college years. Melville was a man of great personal charm, yet he chose during much of his later life to live an isolated and private life, much as Hawthorne and Poe in their different ways did; the consequences of this life are evident in Melville's work. As Edmund Wilson has remarked:

> The voyage of the *Pequod* in *Moby Dick,* for all its variety of incident and its progression to a dramatic end, is a construction of close-knit blocks which have to be surmounted one by one. . . . In the case of all these writers—even Melville and Poe—the relative lack of movement is quite in keeping with the tempo of secluded lives, of men in a position to live by themselves, usually in the country, to write about country manners which they try to think traditional and stable; to idealize historical episodes; to weave fantasies out of their dreams; to reflect upon human life, upon man's relation to Nature, to God and the Universe; to speculate philosophically or euphorically, to burst into impetuous prophecy on the meaning and promise of the United States.

In his intellectual isolation Melville brooded long and hard on his early experiences, wandering insensibly further and further from the customary ideas of his fellow men. In the end he developed an elaborate and highly theoretical structure of personal ideas about what men and societies—especially the democratic society of the United States—ought to be, and in a way very characteristic of natures like his, he became deeply and passionately involved with this idea of the world he had slowly evolved. As a consequence, the mature Melville was a doubting democrat and a reluctant admirer of individualistic intellectual aristocrats like his own Captain Ahab, a skeptical transcendentalist and a shocked admirer of the primitive pagans he had lived with in the South Seas. He had observed something of what seemed to him the natural goodness of man in these savages and among the sailors he had known, and developed a burning anger at the way the institutional structure of society, theoretically made to serve and encourage the natural goodness of men, seemed actually to frustrate and defeat it.

He demanded a great deal of life; he would settle for nothing less than a universe that satisfied completely what he knew to be his expectations of life and believed were the expectations of all mankind. At the same time that he was defining these demands on life, he was becoming more sharply aware of a possibility that decreased radically the chances of his believing any demands on life might be realized. For by the time he came to write *Moby Dick* his ceaseless contemplation of the contrast between what he believed life ought to be and what he had seen it to be in his travels had moved far beyond merely social and political problems to a consideration of the divinely ordained nature of things themselves, which he was coming to fear was blankly indifferent to all of men's needs and desires. "He can," said Hawthorne after meeting Melville on one of his restless wanderings in Liverpool some years after the writing of *Moby Dick,* "neither believe [in the goodness of God] nor be comfortable in his unbelief; and he is too honest and courageous not to try to do one or the other."

Like many other writers of his time—Hawthorne is a good example—Melville wrote in a style that is troublesome, as much because it often attracts as because it sometimes puts off readers by its striking, superficial characteristics. Melville, as Edmund Wilson puts it, "embroidered, or, perhaps better, coagulated, [his] fancies in a peculiarly clogged and viscous prose characteristic of the early nineteenth century, that is [marked by] a self-conscious archaizing, a magniloquence which, though sometimes facetious, has little in common with the eighteenth century; and both have some connection with the romantic movement."

There is always something wrong with a writer's chosing a style for itself, because something about it attracts him regardless of what it expresses, but the habit of doing so has been almost constant among great American writers; Melville and his generation are not the only ones whose work is awkward in this way. Such later American writers as James and Hemingway and Faulkner also wrote in styles that to some extent exist independently of what they are being used to express in order that they may display certain purely stylistic qualities that have some sort of false but irresistible appeal for the writer.

The style Melville chose in this way—or perhaps, as a man of his period, could not escape—is certainly essentially bad, heavily decorated with deliberately artificial flourishes, frequently syntactically overelaborated to the point of incoherence, and, in its diction, often ludicrously inappropriate to the characters and the occasions. The best that can be said in its defense is probably that Melville was trying to escape the elevated and lifeless conventional style of his time, to find something closer to actual speech, without losing the resources for eloquent and passionate assertion that he so badly needed. Despite the intrinsic falseness of his chosen style, Melville manages a good deal of the time, by the sheer intensity of his commitment to what he is trying to express, to be genuinely eloquent. In order to see and experience this eloquence, the reader must come to terms with his style by accepting it—when it is merely clumsy—as an unavoidable limitation imposed on Melville by his period, and by being alert for the ways Melville often managed, despite his style's intrinsic faults, to make it expressive and moving.

Melville was as fascinated as any other nineteenth-century romantic by the endless variety and beauty of the natural world, but his habit of speculating endlessly about the meaning of things committed him early to a metaphysical sense of reality. "I am intent," he said in *Mardi*, "upon the essence of things, the mystery that lieth beyond, . . . that which is beneath the seeming." Thus, even before he wrote *Moby Dick*, Melville had moved toward that absolute distinction between the essence of things and their physical embodiments that was to reduce him in his later years to despairing silence. This habit of thought Mr. Allen Tate has called the fallacy of the angelic imagination—that is, the belief that men can, as angels can, see past the physical natures of things and, by the exercise of their intellects, penetrate directly to essences. This fallacy was a constant danger for a certain kind of transcendentalist, as Edgar Allan Poe's addiction to it shows.

But when Melville wrote *Moby Dick,* the greatest of all his novels and probably the most impressive single work in American literature, the essences of things were still organically embodied for him in the physical particulars of the sensible world. Nonetheless, even in *Moby Dick*—because he was convinced that "some certain significance lurks in all things, else all things are little worth, and the round world itself but an empty cipher, except to sell by cartloads, as they do hills about Boston, to fill up some morass in the Milky Way"—he dealt with the sensible world in a highly metaphysical way. "My dear sir," he says wryly to the reader in the middle of *Moby Dick,* "in this world it is not easy to settle these plain things. I have ever found your plain things the knottiest of all." "Your plain things" were always for him allegories of man's subjective, ethical life; and the possibility that nature might not be imbued with a consciousness like man's own but only blankly inhuman was unbearable to his imagination. "O Nature, O soul of man," he exclaims in *Moby Dick,* "how far beyond all utterance are your linked analogies! not the smallest atom stirs or lives on matter, but has its cunning duplicate in mind."

The book that grew out of this intensely metaphysical but still organic sense of the universe—one Melville was never to achieve again —is a marvelous adventure story. It describes the cruise of a Nantucket whaler, the *Pequod,* under the command of a strange, impressive captain named Ahab. Once the *Pequod* has sailed, it quickly becomes clear that Ahab has no real interest in a profitable catch of whales. He is obsessed by a desire to seek out and kill a famous and elusive albino whale called Moby Dick. The *Pequod* pursues Moby Dick halfway round the world, only to be destroyed by him with the loss of every man aboard except the one—Ishmael—who returns to tell the tale. Melville embodies in every detail of this story his subtle, impassioned metaphysical quarrel, not so much—as Professor Laurence Thompson has put it—with God, as with the exaggerated expectations of life that had become habitual with him as a result of his long, lonely speculating on the nature of things. *Moby Dick* is a book filled with vivid characters that are, even the least significant of them, intensely alive. There is, for example, the Nantucket landlady who serves her boarders nothing but chowder and is full of crotchets. She refuses to allow harpooners to take their harpoons to their rooms, though to do so was almost like taking a gun-fighter's guns from him. Her explanation is gruesomely comic.

> "Ever since young Stiggs coming from that unfort'nt v'y'ge of his, [she says] when he was gone for four years and a half, with only three barrels of *ile,* was found dead in my first floor back, with his harpoon in his side; ever since then I allow no boarders to take sich dangerous weepons in their rooms at night. So . . . I will just take this here iron, and keep it for you till morning. But the chowder; clam or cod to-morrow for breakfast, men?"

Or there is the Shaker from Niskayuna, a town near Albany that Melville must have known. This Shaker is a great prophet, having, as Melville says, "several times descended from heaven by way of a trap-door [in the Shaker meeting house], announcing the speedy opening of the seventh vial, which he carried in his vest pocket." This madman gets himself aboard a whaler called the *Jeroboam,* where he reveals himself to be the archangel Gabriel. His eloquence and sincerity over-awe the crew, and they so terrorize the captain in his defense that he takes effective command of the cruise. He is Melville's grimly comic reminder to himself of how near to madness unrestrained metaphysical speculation is, a parody of *Moby Dick's* central figure, Captain Ahab.

Melville tells his story with a wealth of imagery and allusion that charges it with daring implications every moment, as when, with hair-raising casualness, he describes a school of sharks attacking a whale and "thirstily drinking [the whale's blood] at every new gash, as the eager Israelites did at the bursting fountains that poured from the smitten rocks,"—a figure that makes the sharks naturally innocent in their brutality and the Israelites brutally greedy in their spirituality. It is the blending of vivid natural description and metaphysical im-plication like this that makes possible the great, haunting chapter called "The Grand Armada," where, in the center of a frantic whirl-pool of hundreds of whales, the hunters come to a place of absolute calm and, looking down into the clear waters of the Pacific, see an astonishing sight.

. . . far beneath this wondrous world upon the surface, another and still stranger world met our eyes as we gazed over the side. For, suspended in those watery vaults, floated the forms of the nursing mothers of the whales, and those that by their enormous girth seemed shortly to become mothers. The lake, as I have hinted, was to a considerable depth exceedingly transparent; and as human infants while suckling will calmly and fixedly gaze away from the breast, as if leading two different lives at the time; and while yet drawing mortal nourishment, be still spiritually feasting upon some unearthly reminiscence;—even so did the young of these whales seem looking up towards us, but not at us, as if we were but a bit of Gulf-weed in their new-born sight. . . .

And thus, though surrounded by circle upon circle of consterna-tions and affrights, did these inscrutable creatures at the centre freely and fearlessly indulge in all peaceful concernments; yea, serenely revelling in dalliance and delight. But even so, amid the tornadoed Atlantic of my being, do I myself still for ever cen-trally disport in mute calm; and while ponderous planets of un-waning woe revolve round me, deep down and deep inland there I still bathe me in eternal mildness of joy.

"The Grand Armada," taken as a whole, is a magnificent scene, and it is not the only scene of its kind in *Moby Dick*. There is—to give just one other example—the scene of the sermon in the Nantucket church of Father Mapple, the whalers' priest, with its climactic and terrifying hymn:

> The ribs and terrors in the whale,
>   Arched over me a dismal gloom,
> While all God's sun-lit waves rolled by,
>   And lift me deepening down to gloom.

As Melville put it later in *Moby Dick*, "Though in many of its aspects this visible world seems formed in love, the invisible spheres were formed in fright."

One can feel the power of the agonizing metaphysical tension of Father Mapple's hymn even in the quiet voice of Ishmael, the lonely wanderer who is Melville's spokesman; it is there in the book's very first paragraph.

> Call me Ishmael! Some years ago—never mind how long precisely—having little or no money in my purse, and nothing particular to interest me on shore, I thought I would sail about a little and see the watery part of the world. It is a way I have of driving off the spleen, and regulating the circulation. Whenever I find myself growing grim about the mouth; whenever it is damp, drizzly November in my soul; whenever I find myself involuntarily pausing before coffin warehouses, and bringing up the rear of every funeral I meet; and especially whenever my hypos get such an upper hand of me, that it requires a strong moral principle to prevent me from deliberately stepping into the street, and methodically knocking people's hats off—then, I account it high time to get to sea as soon as I can. This is my substitute for pistol and ball. With a philosophical flourish Cato throws himself upon his sword; I quietly take to the ship. There is nothing surprising in this. If they but knew it, almost all men in their degree, some time or other, cherish very nearly the same feelings toward the ocean with me.

This is the voice that tells us the story of Captain Ahab's enraged voyage in search of Moby Dick, the white whale, a search that takes him and his crew halfway round the world to their deaths. What are its metaphysical implications? At one point during the voyage, in the middle of a whale-hunt, their ship, the *Pequod,* has the head of a sperm whale hanging from the tackle on one side and the head of a right whale hanging from the tackle on the other, and Melville remarks: "So, when on one side you hoist in Locke's head, you go over that way; but now, on the other side, hoist in Kant's and you come back again; but in very poor plight." This is Melville's image of his own plight in a world in which his native land was the latest and most literal attempt to realize the ideal society envisioned in the Lockian political theories of the Enlightenment, with their assumptions that man's reason is adequate to all occasions and that it would eventually discover the whole truth and realize man's happiness in a perfected society. Melville himself accepted these assumptions—or at least did not know how to make sense of the world without accepting them.

But then there was Kant's head. Melville saw much in human experience beyond what reason, as the Enlightenment of the eighteenth century conceived it, could grasp. Like Hawthorne, he was acutely conscious of the supernatural, of a mysterious, incomprehensible power in the universe that appeared to him to be omnipotent and therefore irresistible, but, at the same time, unendurable in its appalling indifference to the evil and suffering in the world it had created and ruled over. Like the *Pequod* rolling from one side to the other as first the head of the sperm whale and then the head of the right whale were hoisted up, Melville was "in very poor plight," between the drag of Locke's head and the drag of Kant's—between the rational social optimism that was the political inheritance of his society and the gloomy pessimism about man's ultimate fate that was the religious inheritance of his society.

Sometimes he expressed this plight in the quiet voice of Ishmael, who observes at one point, "Long exile from Christendom and civilization inevitably restores a man to that condition in which God placed him, i.e., what is called savagery; I myself am a savage." Beneath the casual tone of that remark there is a grim and terrible irony. Man's proper condition, the condition God has designed for him, is savagery, which—denial though it is of all the values of Christian civilization— Melville has discovered provides a more honorable and endurable life than does the nominally Christian civilization he had observed in the slums of Liverpool and in the American Navy. Long exile—the bold adventure across what are for Melville as much seas of thought as of salt water—"inevitably *restores*" man to his divinely ordained condition, that is, savagery, a state that is, when it is measured against the ideals of Christian civilization, degraded, but is, when it is measured against the actual conduct of the society Melville saw around him, distinctly superior. What is so shocking about this irony is the violent, suppressed emotional strain between Melville's response to the promises of Christian and civilized life and his consciousness of society's actual, brutal indifference to these promises; and this irony is given tragic force by his certainty that, whatever life is, God has made it so.

These are the feelings that drive Captain Ahab mad. He refuses to believe that the evils of the world cannot be eradicated by a man who is determined enough and will travel far enough to find and destroy them. He is democracy's epic hero. But Melville was fully aware that in making Captain Ahab seek to destroy the evil of the world, he was making him challenge God and seek to destroy a part of His creation—was assuming that man is as great as God Himself and therefore able—indeed, morally obligated—to call God to account. Yet Melville never for a moment doubted God's omnipotence or the consequent indestructibility of His creation. "Away, ye chattering apes of a sophomorean Spinoza and Plato," he says in *Pierre*. ". . . Explain this darkness, exorcise this devil, ye cannot." Thus, though the world was unbearable to Melville as long as it was possessed by this devil, and though his heart went out to Ahab and his Promethean defiance of God, he was quite sure that Ahab's defiance was hopeless, was, finally, a madness.

Ahab will inevitably be defeated by that aspect of the divinely ordained universe embodied for Melville in Leviathan, the huge, irresistibly powerful, mindless white whale, Moby Dick. But Ahab will not accept the possibility that he cannot dominate and remake with his intelligence God's universe in accordance with his own wishes. At most he has occasional dark moments of doubting that God—good or evil—is present in the universe at all.

> "Hark ye yet again,—[he says to his mate Starbuck] the little lower layer. All visible objects, man, are but as pasteboard masks. But in each event—in the living act, the undoubted deed—there, some unknown but still reasoning thing puts forth the mouldings of its features from behind the unreasoning mask. If man will

strike, strike through the mask! How can the prisoner reach outside except by thrusting through the wall? To me, the white whale
is that wall, shoved near to me. Sometimes I think there's naught
behind. But 'tis enough. He tasks me; he heaps me; I see in him
outrageous strength, with an inscrutable malice sinewing it. That
inscrutable thing is chiefly what I hate; and be the white whale
agent, or be the white whale principal, I will wreak that hate upon
him. Talk not to me of blasphemy, man; I'd strike the sun if it
insulted me. . . . Who's over me? Truth hath no confines."

This American Prometheus has his incidental personal motives;
Moby Dick has taken one of his legs off during a previous voyage.
But his deepest purpose is to defy the nature of things for the benefit
of his fellow men. Like all great leaders, he knows his fellow men have
not his strength of purpose, knows that he must concentrate himself
on his objective at the expense of his personal relations with them
(early in the voyage he even throws away his pipe, the last reminder
of his everyday humanity). He knows, indeed, that he must command
his crew—often against their own wishes—in order that they may
serve him in his quest for their good. "And when these things unite
in a man of greatly superior natural force," says Melville of Ahab,
"with a globular brain and a ponderous heart; who has also by the
stillness and seclusion of many long night-watches in the remotest
waters, and beneath constellations never seen here at the north, been
led to think untraditionally and independently . . . that man makes
one in a whole nation's census—a mighty pageant creature, formed
for noble tragedies. Nor will it at all detract from him, dramatically
regarded, if either by birth or circumstances, he have what seems a
half wilful over-ruling morbidness at the bottom of his nature. For
all men tragically great are made so through a certain morbidness. Be
sure of this, O young ambition, all mortal greatness is but disease."

Thus Ahab's monomaniacal commitment to his mission in the
world—the conquest of Moby Dick and all he represents in order that
a just, humane, and democratic world may come into existence—destroys in him all fellow feeling, all possibility of loving the humanity

in whose service he is ostensibly sacrificing himself. Ahab becomes, as Melville says, "inaccessible. Though nominally included in the census of Christendom, he was still an alien to it. He lived in the world, as the last of the Grisly Bears lived in settled Missouri. And as when Spring and Summer had departed, lived out the winter there, sucking his own paws; so, in his inclement, howling old age, Ahab's soul, shut up in the caved trunk of his body, there fed upon the sullen paws of its gloom!"

Still, for that part of Melville's mind that is symbolized by Locke's head, the part that believed in the final significance of the needs and desires of the individual soul regardless of what the inscrutable, omnipotent power that rules the universe seems to decree, Ahab is right and his life is heroic; he is, as Peleg says, "a grand, ungodly, godlike man" who defies God by asserting the divinity of man. Starbuck, Ahab's mate and the unimaginative, conventionally good man of the book, sees Ahab's magnanimity even as he is convinced of Ahab's madness.

My soul [he says] is more than matched [by Ahab]; she is overmanned; and by a madman! Insufferable sting, that sanity should ground arms on such a field! But he drilled deep down, and blasted all my reason out of me! I think I see his impious end; but feel that I must help him to it. Will I, nill I, the ineffable thing has tied me to him; tows me with a cable I have no knife to cut. Horrible old man! Who's over him, he cries; aye, he would be a democrat to all above; look how he lords over all below! Oh! I plainly see my miserable office,—to obey, rebelling; and worse yet, to hate with touch of pity! For in his eyes I read some lurid woe would shrivel me up, had I it.

This, then, is Melville's tragic hero, the man who damns himself by his refusal to accept the creation as God has made it, who remains to the end heroically defiant of an omnipotent God Melville himself believes to the end has mismade the world by making it indifferent to the precious personal consciousness of man.

"I now know thee, thou clear spirit, [Ahab says to God near the end of his voyage] and I now know that thy right worship is defiance. To neither love nor reverence wilt thou be kind; and e'en for hate thou canst but kill; and all are killed. No fearless fool now fronts thee. I own thy speechless, placeless power; but to the last gasp of my earthquake life will dispute its unconditional, unintegral mastery of me. In the midst of the personified impersonal, a personality stands here. Though but a point at best; whencesoe'er I came; wheresoe'er I go; yet while I earthly live, the queenly personality lives in me, and feels her royal rights. But war is pain, and hate is woe. Come in the lowest form of love, and I will kneel and kiss thee; but at thy highest, come as mere supernal power; and though thou launchest navies of full-freighted worlds, there's that here that still remains indifferent. Oh, thou clear spirit, of thy fire thou madest me, and like a true child of fire, I breathe it back at thee."

Melville chose the story of a whaling captain's voyage for this fable of man's fate because it was at once homely and magnificent; whalers sailed every season in fleets from New Bedford and Nantucket, set forth on their world-girdling voyages in heroic pursuit of the largest and most terrifying of God's creatures. And by means of his ingenious and grimly gothic humor, he managed to suggest some sort of similarity between that voyage and nearly every other Promethean myth in Western culture; he even gets in St. George, whose dragon, he suggests, was really a whale, adding,

. . . by good rights, we harpooners of Nantucket should be enrolled in the most noble order of St. George. And therefore, let not the knights of that honorable company (none of whom, I venture to say, have ever had to do with a whale like our great patron), let them never eye Nantucketers with disdain, since even in our woollen frocks and tarred trowsers we are much better entitled to St. George's decoration than they.

Thus, with a complexity of irony that seems to reverberate endlessly, Melville makes the world's hero out of the common man, out of the *Pequod's* shipload of Nantucketers and Manxmen, South Sea-

D

island savages and Negroes in their woollen frocks and tarred trowsers—his "Anacharsis Clootz [Clootz was a violent egalitarian of the French Revolution] deputation from all the isles of the sea and all the ends of the earth [that accompanied] old Ahab in the *Pequod* to lay the world's grievances before that bar from which not many of them come back."

Men [Melville says] may seem detestable as joint stock companies and nations; knaves, fools, and murderers there may be; men may have mean and meagre faces; but man, in the ideal, is so noble and so sparkling, such a grand and glowing creature, that over any ignominious blemish in him all his fellows should run to throw their costliest robes. That immaculate manliness we feel within ourselves, so far within us, that it remains intact though all the outer character seem gone; bleeds with keenest anguish at the undraped spectacle of a valor-ruined man. Nor can piety itself, at such a shameful sight, completely stifle her upbraidings against the permitting stars. But this august dignity I treat of, is not the dignity of kings and robes, but that abounding dignity which has no robed investiture. Thou shalt see it shining in the arm that wields a pick or drives a spike; that democratic dignity which, on all hands, radiates without end from God; Himself! The great God Absolute! The centre and circumference of all democracy! His omnipresence, our divine equality!

In Melville's mythologizing of the whale-hunt conducted under Ahab's leadership by the divinely democratic crew of the *Pequod,* the sperm whale, with its huge, broad head, is the image of the "dread powers" of the divine; but, Melville adds, "the head of this Leviathan, in the creature's living intact state, is an entire delusion. As for his true brain, you can see no indication of it, nor feel any. The whale, like all things that are mighty, wears a false brow to the common world. . . . And by these negations, considered along with the affirmative fact of his prodigious bulk and power, you can best form to yourself the truest, though not the most exhilarating conception of what the most exalted potency is"—a potency, the reader is not to forget, that includes not only the mighty of the world but omnipotent

God Himself. The rare albino sperm whale, Moby Dick, is in his whiteness at once the most awesome and the most terrifying of these natural images of God's omnipotence. The awful indefiniteness of that white horrifies Melville. "It is," he says, "at once the most meaning symbol of spiritual things, nay, the very veil of the Christian's Deity; and yet should be as it is, the intensifying agent in things the most appalling to mankind. Is it that by its indefiniteness it shadows forth the heartless voids and immensities of the universe, and thus stabs us from behind with the thought of annihilation, when beholding the white depths of the milky way?"

With that incredibly powerful white brow of his, behind which there is no brain, no possibility of meaning at all, Moby Dick finally crushes the *Pequod* and destroys all its crew except Ishmael, who escapes to report to us Melville's terrible vision of the ribs and terrors of the whale which, though God's sunlit waves roll by, lifts us all deepening down to doom.

MARK TWAIN
1835-1910

Huckleberry Finn
1882

The two great writers who dominate American fiction in the second
half of the nineteenth century, Mark Twain and Henry James, remind
us afresh of the conflicting aspects of reality that are evident in the
work of Cooper and Hawthorne at the beginning of the century. Like
them Twain and James divide on this question. For Twain reality lies
in man's relations with his society, in how he acts as a social being
and in his reasons for acting that way. He can dramatize the conduct
and motives of his characters in a book like *Huckleberry Finn* very
beautifully, but it is the ironic clash of public attitudes and ideas—
ideas about slavery and social convention and wealth—that interests
him, not the shifts of mood and feeling within his characters that constitute the actual life of their consciousness.

James, on the other hand, had, as T. S. Eliot once wryly put it, "a
mind so fine that no idea could violate it." Eliot meant this quite seriously, as indeed he should have. He calls it "the last test of a superior
intelligence," the one that makes James "the most intelligent man of
his generation" and distinguishes him from most of the rest of us,
who "corrupt our feelings with ideas; [who] produce the political, the
emotional ideas, evading sensation and thought." James's novels never

focus on the substance of political and social conflicts and the ideas involved in them, even when he is ostensibly concerned with them, as he is for large parts of *The Bostonians* and *The Princess Casamassima*. His interest is always in the inner natures of his characters and the drama of the conflict between them.

At first glance, moreover, Twain and James may appear so unlike that it is hard to believe they could have been products of the same time and place. James was a cosmopolitan man of great culture who moved with stately dignity through the best society of England and America, and Mark Twain was a redheaded, hot-tempered, hard-swearing, whiskey-drinking roughneck who spent the significant years of his life in frontier mining camps and wrote books like *The Innocents Abroad* in which he laughed with ignorant complacency at everything Henry James held dear. Nevertheless the two had more in common than appears at first glance, as one can guess if he reminds himself that though Henry James came of a wealthy and cultivated New York family, his grandfather had been a penniless Irish immigrant, and that though Mark Twain grew up in poverty on the American frontier, his mother's family was obsessed by the idea that they were connected with the earls of Durham. Twain could make glorious fun of this notion, as he does with Colonel Sellers in *The Gilded Age,* but the impulse it represented was nonetheless in him.

Still, Twain was no "lone wolf prowling the forests of the intellect," but a frontiersman. He grew up in the remote, primitive, Mississippi River village of Hannibal, Missouri—the St. Petersburg of *Huckleberry Finn.* He had almost no formal education, but all his life he was an omnivorous reader, and he cultivated his sense of American English—a language in which he was a virtuoso of style—as a journeyman printer and newspaper reporter. After wandering the country for several years picking up odd jobs, he settled down for three years in the late 1850's to become a riverboat pilot, an experience that gave him the material for *Life on the Mississippi,* which was written at much the same time as *Huckleberry Finn* and is, apart from it, the most wonderful of all his books. But he was soon off again, wandering to the Nevada Territory and to a job as a reporter in the famous mining town of Virginia City; thence, at the suggestion of Bret Harte, he went to San Francisco, where he published his first successful piece of fiction, an early version of "The Celebrated Jumping Frog of Calaveras County." Characteristically, he had picked up the story in a dingy bar in Angel's Camp, California.

From this start he rose rapidly to wide popular fame and considerable wealth and promptly set about earnestly to make himself over into a proper Victorian gentleman. Despite subsequent constant, sentimental efforts to make it appear that the real Mark Twain was bullied into silence by the Victorian prissiness of his close friend, the novelist William Dean Howells, and his wife, Olivia, there is every evidence that it was Mark Twain himself—or a part of him—that dictated this effort at change. It is true that another part of him always shared with Huck Finn a dislike of efforts to civilize him, and in fact his beloved Livy never did cure him of his violent outbursts of temper and swearing or his habit of keeping himself healthy with copious and frequent doses of whiskey. Nor did he ever quite succeed in subduing the habit of throwing into his life a lot of style, as Huck Finn puts it about Tom Sawyer—an ungenteel tendency to flamboyance that is represented by Mark Twain's brilliantly white suits, worn in defiance of the universal Victorian black broadcloth, his great bush of unruly red—and later white—hair, his addiction to ungentlemanly and even bawdy stories told in an exaggerated frontier drawl.

Nevertheless, it was he, not Olivia Langdon, who was determined that this gentle invalid daughter of a wealthy businessman should marry and reform him; it was he who was bent on building their large and tasteful Gothic mansion in the fashionable Nook Farm area of Hartford, Connecticut, with its "permanent polychrome" exterior, its elegant interior decoration, its seven bathrooms. The Mark Twain who, on discovering a button missing from a shirt, stood at the bedroom window of this mansion, swearing like the Mississippi Riverman he partly was and throwing every shirt he owned onto the meticulously trimmed lawns below, was a complicated—and representative

—American mixture of frontiersman and gentleman, of Noble Savage and Intellectual, and this mixture is evident in every aspect of his nature.

He hated bitterly the grossly dishonest business life of his time and the political corruption it induced; yet he was an incurably eager, wildly speculative businessman, fascinated by the commercial possibilities of impractical inventions like the mechanical typesetter into which he poured so much money that despite his immense earnings as a writer and lecturer, he was driven into bankruptcy in 1894. He was a bitter pessimist of some amateur philosophical pretensions and at the same time a man with an irrepressible, spontaneous delight in life. He was enraged by social injustice, particularly the social injustice of slavery, and the model of gentility he set himself was that of the Southern gentleman. It is typical of him to have combined with his anarchistic concern for civil liberties a favorite scheme for giving extra votes to men of intellectual attainments *and* to men of wealth.

A warm-hearted, impulsive man, avid of success and fame, he had little appreciation of the difference between his great work and his literary journalism: he seems to have thought for a long time that *Huckleberry Finn,* one of the world's great books, was just another boys' book like *Tom Sawyer.* But when some accident released the full powers of his imagination, as it did for all but the final section of *Huckleberry Finn,* he could produce the most powerful image of the American's sense of the world he lives in that we have.

Huckleberry Finn is a first-person narrative, told with all Huck's profound and comically literal-minded honesty in the dialect of his place and time. The choice of this method of narration solved at a stroke the vexed problem of style, for Twain was an expert at the dialects of the region he was writing about. He was rightly proud of this knowledge; he even has a note at the beginning of *Huckleberry Finn* that tells the reader how expert the rendering of dialect in the novel is. But as with so many things in *Huckleberry Finn,* the reader is not entirely sure Twain saw how much his use of this dialect really did for his novel. Huck's speech gives his story a normal and convincing tone of voice that is extremely effective for describing action; but, because Twain knew his dialect so well, he was also able to make it serve his own humor and irony without—save on rare occasions—making the reader aware that it is really Twain, rather than any possible Huck, who is speaking.

At the end of *Tom Sawyer,* Huck had acquired a fortune of six thousand dollars; it causes him endless trouble. The good people of St. Petersburg immediately set about to rescue him from the glorious freedom of the tramp's life he has so far lived, and Huck finds this civilizing process very painful, though he understands how well-meant it is.

The widow she cried over me, and called me a poor lost lamb, and she called me a lot of other names, too, but she never meant no harm by it. She put me in them new clothes . . . and I couldn't do nothing but sweat and sweat, and feel all cramped up. Well, then, the old thing commenced again. The widow rung a bell for supper, and you had to come to time. When you got to table you couldn't go right to eating, but you had to wait for the widow to tuck down her head and grumble a little over the victuals, though there warn't really anything the matter with them—that is, nothing only everything was cooked by itself. In a barrel of odds and ends it is different; things get mixed up, and the juice kind of swaps around, and things go better.

After supper she got out her book and learned me about Moses and the Bulrushers, and I was in a sweat to find out all about him; but by and by she let it out that Moses had been dead a considerable time; so then I didn't care no more about him, because I don't take no stock in dead people.

Pretty soon I wanted to smoke, and asked the widow to let me. But she wouldn't. She said it was a mean practice and wasn't clean, and I must try not to do it any more. That is just the way with some people. They get down on a thing when they don't know nothing about it. Here she was a-bothering about Moses, which was no kin to her, and no use to anybody, being gone, you see, yet finding a power of fault with me for doing a thing that had some good in it. And she took snuff, too; of course that was all right, because she done it herself.

But presently Huck is kidnapped and carried off from civilization to a cabin across the river by his drunken father, who wants Huck's six thousand dollars. Huck quite enjoys the life, despite his father's brutality, but then his father, in a bout of delirium tremens, tries to kill him and he runs away to a deserted island down river. There he encounters a slave named Jim who has run away from the widow's family because they plan to sell him down river, the worst fate possible for a slave. Without much thought, Huck joins forces with him and they start floating down the river looking for Cairo, Illinois, where the Ohio River joins the Mississippi. If Jim can get up the Ohio into the North, he can be free. But they drift past Cairo in a fog. Meanwhile, Huck has been listening to Jim's excited talk about what he will do when he is free and it has disturbed what Huck calls his conscience.

Conscience says to me, "What had poor Miss Watson done to you that you could see her nigger go off right under your eyes and never say one single word? What did that poor woman do to you that you could treat her so mean?" . . . Jim talked out loud all the time I was talking to myself. He was saying how the first thing he would do when he got to a free state he would go to saving up his money and never spend a single cent, and when he got enough he would buy his wife, which was owned on a farm close to where Miss Watson lived; and then they would both work to buy the two children, and if their master wouldn't sell them, they'd get an Ab'litionist to go and steal them.

It most froze me to hear such talk. He wouldn't ever dared to talk such talk in his life before. . . . Thinks I, this is what comes of my not thinking. Here was this nigger, which I had as good as helped to run away, coming right out flat-footed and saying he would steal his children—children that belonged to a man I didn't even know; a man that hadn't ever done me no harm.

The powerful irony of this passage is made possible by the naïveté of Huck. Only a mind of the greatest literalness could be convincingly represented as looking at this naked confrontation of what Huck calls "conscience"—that is, the belief in the inhuman rights of investors in slaves not to be deprived of their property without due process which has been drilled by Huck's society into every one of its members, even the otherwise free tramp like Huck—and the "natural," human rights of Jim, as a man, to love his wife and yearn for his children. This second element in the conflict is only made more moving by the Victorian virtues Twain ascribes to Jim—the middle-class domesticity of his feelings about his wife and children, his almost Horatio Algier determination to work and save up his money and never spend a single cent in order to buy his children out of slavery. The final plan he considers, getting "an Ab'litionist to go and steal" his children if their owner refuses to sell them, is a measure of how much he loves these children. It is quite beautiful that his consideration of this plan should be the final shock to Huck's conscience that awakens him to the wickedness of consorting with Jim and of even as good as helping him to run away from the kindly and well-meaning (but not harmless) Miss Watson—as in fact, of course, she really is, whether she is holding Jim in chattel slavery or Huck in the more subtle slavery of civilized deportment that requires him to "set up straight" and not "gap and stretch" and generally behave in a wholly unnatural way.

When Huck's conscience is thus badly shaken by Jim's wicked talk of stealing his children from an innocent owner, he decides it is his moral duty to betray Jim. This decision is a great relief to him, and the minute they sight a town he sets off in the canoe to find somebody to capture Jim. Unluckily, as he is leaving Jim says to him, "I'se a free man, en I couldn't ever been free ef it hadn' been for Huck . . . you's de bes' fren' Jim's ever had; en you's de *only* fren' ole Jim's got now." This innocent expression of human affection and gratitude is very ill-timed for poor Huck; as he says, "I was paddling off, all in a sweat to tell on him; but when he says this, it seemed to kind of take the tuck all out of me." As a result, when he comes on some men in a canoe who are actually looking for runaway slaves (though as it happens not Jim) Huck finds he is not "man enough" to betray Jim. Instead he finds himself inventing and performing with great skill a complicated lie that persuades the men in the canoe not to go near the raft where Jim is hiding: he makes them believe—he never says so himself—that there are three people with smallpox on the raft.

He is deeply discouraged to find himself acting this way, as if he "hadn't the spunk of a rabbit." "I knowed very well," he says, "that I had done wrong, and I see it warn't no use for me to try to learn to do right; a body that don't get *started* right when he's little ain't got no show—when the pinch comes there ain't nothing to back him up and keep him to his work, and so he gets beat. . . . So I reckoned I wouldn't bother no more about it, but after this always do whichever came handiest at the time."

Thus the central moral conflict of the novel is brought into focus, and the point of the passage is not just the horror of slavery, for all Twain's angry irony about it. As much of the rest of the novel shows, Twain had almost equally serious doubts of the adequacy, as a moral program, of doing whatever comes handiest at the time. He clearly thought that if the moral standards of organized society are usually a tyrannical if largely unconscious hypocrisy, the moral standards of the natural man are equally subject to corruption by ego and self-interest. Huck's Pap is a terrifying image of how ignoble the savage can be. Pap's drunken harangue to Huck when he finds it impossible to get hold of Huck's six thousand dollars is a masterpiece of natural moral ugliness.

> "Call this a govment! [he says] why, just look at it and see what it's like. Here's the law a-standing ready to take a man's son away from him—a man's own son, which he has had all the trouble and all the anxiety and all the expense of raising. Yes, just as that man has got that son raised at last, and ready to go to work and begin to do suthin' for *him* and give him a rest, the law up and goes for him. And they call *that* govment! That ain't all, nuther. The law backs that old Judge Thatcher up and helps him to keep me out o' my property. Here's what the law does: the law takes a man worth six thousand dollars and up'ards, and jams him into an old trap of a cabin like this, and lets him go round in clothes that ain't fitten for a hog. They call that govment! . . .

"Why, looky here. There was a free nigger there from Ohio—
a mulatter, most as white as a white man. He had the whitest shirt
on you ever see, too, and the shiniest hat; and there ain't a man in
that town that's got as fine clothes as what he had; and he had a
gold watch and chain, and a silver-headed cane—the awfulest old
gray-headed nabob in the state. And what do you think? They
said he was a p'fessor in a college, and could talk all kinds of languages, and knowed everything. And that ain't the wust. They
said he could *vote* when he was at home. Well, that let me out.
Thinks I, what is the country a-coming to? It was 'lection day,
and I was just about to go and vote myself if I warn't too drunk
to get there; but when they told me there was a state in this country where they'd let that nigger vote, I drawed out. I says I'll never
vote ag'in. Them's the very words I said; they all heard me; and
the country may rot for all of me—I'll never vote ag'in as long as
I live. And to see the cool way of that nigger—why, he wouldn't
'a' give me the road if I hadn't shoved him out o' the way."

There are marvelous touches here. In his desire to get his hands on
Huck's six thousand dollars and to have Huck work so he can rest,
Pap has persuaded himself that he has been to a great deal of trouble
and anxiety and expense to raise a son for whom he has in fact never
done anything at all. It is a beautiful demonstration of how naturally
and easily a man can take the word for the deed in the conduct of his
own life when he is motivated by that most natural of human impulses, greed. Pap's attitude toward the Negro professor is equally
pure, and simple in motive. Twain of course means us to see this professor as altogether admirable, the model Negro; the fine clothes, the
gold watch and chain, the silver-headed cane, show him to have the
wealth Twain thought desirable in a ruling class, as the knowledge of
languages shows him to have the intellect Twain also thought desirable in this class. Pap naturally hates both kinds of merit equally, and
it is quite wonderful the way he threatens the country with the loss of
his patronage—"I'll never vote ag'in . . . the country may rot for all
of me"—if it continues to allow well-to-do and intelligent Negroes to
vote. His motive is as evident as is his conviction of its righteousness:

he is determined to take the road of all niggers, and the greater their merits, the greater the credit to him for doing so.

As the anarchic natural man—and as such the true father of the equally anarchic natural man, Huck—Pap is as opposed to the orderly and lawful conduct of organized society as Huck is, but his reasons for being so are as selfish and inconsiderate as Huck's are loving and thoughtful. His attitudes toward both Huck and the Negroes are as inhuman as those of organized society in St. Petersburg, without having anything of St. Petersburg's saving innocence of motive about them. The life of the natural man is not a safe alternative to the life of organized society (is in fact often worse), except when the natural man is still an innocent child—but then the innocent child of organized society, as represented by Tom Sawyer, is basically good too. Neither Huck nor Tom ever goes astray except when some idea inculcated by civilized society misleads him for a moment, as Huck is momentarily misled by what he has been taught to think about slavery and Tom by his education, his reading of what Twain thought viciously romantic novels. But Pap never fails to go wrong, and organized society only rarely fails to do so.

Twain's inability to see that *Huckleberry Finn* is a far finer book than *Tom Sawyer* suggests that he did not consciously prefer Huck to Tom—or at least that if the riverman in Twain did prefer Huck, the squire of Nook Farm preferred Tom. Even in *Huckleberry Finn,* Tom Sawyer is clearly meant to be a more sympathetic character than he is thought to be by most modern readers, who dislike him more than Twain did. Even if it be true that, whether Twain consciously recognized it or not, he preferred the innocence of the natural child to the innocence of the civilized one, the important thing to notice is that it is the innocence of both that matters—not whether they are natural or civilized but whether they are children or adults. That innocence does not survive maturity; neither the civilized adults of St. Petersburg nor the uncivilized natural man, Pap, has it.

In order to be free to live the innocent natural life Huck must escape both the tyranny of St. Petersburg and the tyranny of Pap. He does so by fleeing to the humanly neutral, natural world of the great, powerful, solemn river. He cannot exist there very long. For one thing, the river is constantly being invaded by men like the Duke and the Dauphin who combine the worst features of nature and civilization. For another, Huck is always being drawn back to life on land by his yearning for human society. Life on the river is, as Huck says, "powerful lonesome." The conflict between Huck's feelings about the river —his sense of the awesome grandeur of the world it makes him free in and his sense of its intolerable loneliness—is evident from the first moment he escapes to it from the cabin his father has locked him in.

One can see Huck's love of the river and his sense of its intolerable lonesomeness in any one of Twain's many marvelous evocations of life on the Mississippi. Consider, for example the very first one, which comes just as Huck has escaped from his father and is free and alone for the first time in the book.

> I got out among the driftwood, and then laid down in the bottom of the canoe and let her float. I laid there and had a good rest and a smoke out of my pipe, looking away into the sky; not a cloud in it. The sky looks ever so deep when you lay down on your back in the moonshine; I never knowed it before. And how far a body can hear on the water such nights! I heard people talking at the ferry-landing. I heard what they said, too—every word of it. One man said it was getting towards the long days and the short nights now. T'other one said *this* warn't one of the short ones, he reckoned—and then they laughed, and he said it over again, and they laughed again; then they waked up another fellow and told him, and laughed, but he didn't laugh; he ripped out something brisk, and said let him alone. The first fellow said he 'lowed to tell it to his old woman—she would think it was pretty good; but he said that warn't nothing to some things he had said in his time. I heard one man say it was nearly three o'clock, and he hoped daylight wouldn't wait more than about a week longer. After that the talk got further and further away, and I couldn't make out the words any more; but I could hear the mumble, and now and then a laugh, too, but it seemed a long ways off.

How stupidly dull—and yet how movingly human—is that conversation on the ferry-landing from which the beautiful and inhuman river is taking Huck further and further away.

At the end of Chapter Sixteen, when Huck and Jim have missed Cairo, Twain laid the novel aside for three years, apparently unable to think of any plausible reason why Jim and Huck should float on down the Mississippi deeper and deeper into slave country. Then, in 1880, he thought of the two scoundrels called the Duke and the Dauphin, who take charge of the raft and of Huck and Jim in order to go from village to village working their frauds on the ignorant and greedy inhabitants. This device not only solved the problem of Jim but allowed Twain to write the great central section of the novel, which shows us through Huck's clear and uncynical eyes what the life of organized society is like.

Huck is first driven ashore when a riverboat rams their raft in the dark. He is taken in by a family of Southern aristocrats named Graingerford. They live what seems to Huck a cultivated life in a house more splendid than anything Huck has ever seen before and his description of it is a masterpiece of irony on Twain's part, delicately balanced between his respect for Victorian culture and his sense of its falseness.

I hadn't [says Huck] seen no house out in the country before that was so nice and had so much style. It didn't have an iron latch on the front door, nor a wooden one with a buckskin string, but a brass knob to turn, the same as houses in town. There warn't no bed in the parlor, nor sign of a bed; but heaps of parlors in towns has beds in them. There was a big fireplace that was bricked on the bottom. . . . They had big brass dog-irons that could hold up a saw-log. There was a clock on the middle of the mantelpiece, with a picture of a town painted on the bottom half of the glass front, and a round place in the middle of it for the sun, and you could see the pendulum swinging behind it. It was beautiful to hear that clock tick; and sometimes when one of these peddlers had been along and scoured her up and got her in good shape, she

would start in and strike a hundred and fifty before she got tuck-
ered out. They wouldn't take any money for her. . . .

These Graingerfords are involved in a vicious, meaningless feud
with a neighboring family named Shepherdson; the Shepherdsons
presently kill off all but one of the Graingerford males. Meanwhile
the two families meet only at church.

> The men took their guns . . . and kept them between their knees
> or stood them handy against the wall. The Shepherdsons done the
> same. It was pretty ornery preaching—all about brotherly love,
> and such-like tiresomeness; but everybody said it was a good ser-
> mon, and they all talked it over going home, and had such a pow-
> erful lot to say about faith and good works and free grace and
> preforeordestination, and I don't know what all, that it did seem
> to me one of the roughest Sundays I had run across yet.

In the afternoon Huck returns to the church on an errand. ". . . there
warn't anybody at the church, except maybe a hog or two, for there
warn't any lock on the door, and hogs like a puncheon floor in sum-
mer-time because it's cool. If you notice, most folks don't go to
church only when they've got to; but a hog is different."

When the final battle breaks out between the Graingerfords and
the Shepherdsons, Huck is sickened by the wanton slaughter and flees
to the raft and the river, where the Duke and the Dauphin take him
from village to village, forcing him to assist them in their frauds. The
Dauphin passes himself off as a reformed pirate at a camp-meeting
and collects $87.75; "he said it warn't no use talking, heathens don't
amount to shucks alongside of pirates to work a camp-meeting." Together he and the Duke put on a performance of Shakespeare in one
village and an obscene display called the king's cameleopard in another. These adventures are climaxed by their attempting to pass
themselves off as the English brothers of a villager who has just died,
leaving a considerable property. Like most of these deceptions of the
Duke and Dauphin, this one ends with everyone fleeing for his life.
Finally, having first betrayed poor Jim into captivity for a mere forty

dollars, these two scoundrels try their performance of the king's cameleopard one time too many, and the last Huck sees of them, they are being rushed out of town by a mob, tarred and feathered and riding on rails. In spite of all Huck has suffered from these two, he thinks as he watches them, It made me sick to see it; and I was sorry for them poor pitiful rascals. . . .. It was a dreadful thing to see. Human beings *can* be awful cruel to one another."

By a thoroughly implausible plot device Twain then brings Tom Sawyer to the farm where Jim is being held prisoner and Huck has followed him. Tom organizes an elaborate "adventure" for freeing Jim; in it all the conventional features of hairbreadth escapes in romantic novels are carefully observed. The whole business evidently amused Twain far more than it does most modern readers, who find it much too long, but its point—the essential innocence of Tom and the incongruity between that innocence and the rules of conduct he has learned from books it is necessary for him to follow—ought not to be missed. Tom has, in fact, come all this way out of the goodness of his heart to tell Jim—later, to be sure, rather than sooner—that Jim is legally free; old Miss Watson, dead now, had become so ashamed of her plan to sell Jim down the river that she had instead set him free in her will.

But neither Jim nor we learn this until Tom's Aunt Polly, who has set out in pursuit of him, finally reaches the farm too and takes both him and Huck in hand. Everyone is thus made happy except Huck, who finds himself in exactly the same situation he was in at the start of the book. He cannot endure this situation now any better than he could then, and in the last words of the book he says, "I reckon I got to light out for the territory ahead of the rest, because Aunt Sally she's going to adopt me and civilize me, and I can't stand it. I been there before."

Thus the true Huck Finn passes forever from our sight. Twain made one or two ill-advised and happily abortive efforts to write about him as an adult, but Huck can never be a grown man in a real world. His nature was even more deeply divided than his author's between

E

his yearning for the life of the innocent natural man that he found it nearly impossible to get free for and was too lonesome to endure when he did, and his need for a mature human society that, whenever he was in it, turned out to be unbearably stupid and cruel.

It has often been observed that in *Huckleberry Finn* Twain was describing the lost world of his Mississippi childhood—not the Mississippi world of his own day, or even the real one of his childhood. Beneath the uproarious comedy of *Huckleberry Finn*, that is, there is a tragic pastoral, one of the great visions of the unattainable world we see when we imagine men to be the childlike, innocent, natural creatures that they are assumed to be by the doctrine of the Noble Savage, Western Civilization's perennial secular dream of salvation. That dream has been specially important in American society because it contributed a good deal to the conception of society that inspired the founders of the United States. As a consequence it has been important to American literature, from the time of Cooper's Natty Bumpo to the time of Scott Fitzgerald's incongruously urbanized Huck Finn, Jay Gatsby.

HENRY JAMES
1843-1916

The Ambassadors

1902

Mark Twain once observed that he would rather be consigned to the Puritan heaven than have to read one of Henry James's novels. This is, of course, Mark Twain the popular professional comedian speaking, the Will Rogers of the age of innocence who kept audiences in gales of laughter by posing as the plain American, the innocent abroad, whose native common sense, unblurred by any real understanding of what he was talking about, saw through the elaborate absurdity of high culture. This Mark Twain knew that the people James wrote about and the life they lived were hopelessly trivial. As H. G. Wells, the plain Englishman who was equally bored by James's novels said, James's characters are "eviscerated"; they "never make lusty love, never go to angry war, never shout at an election or perspire at poker."

If such remarks about James's novels have a slightly unpleasant air of complacency, that is because they deliberately appeal to the prejudices of the audience they are meant for, an audience that so much dislikes the means James uses—the upper-class life of refined sensibilities and complicated manners he describes—that it is blind to the purpose they serve, the revelation of an aspect of reality quite as significant as the one Twain reveals by describing innocently savage children like Tom Sawyer and Huckleberry Finn.

This prejudice against James's means goes—or at least went in James's time—very deep in American society, and the habit of judging novels by one's prejudices about their subject matter in general rather than by the truth that subject matter is used to reveal probably goes even deeper. People far more intelligent about James than Twain and Wells were trying to be are sometimes driven by their dislike of gentility into equally irresponsible jokes about James's novels. Henry's brother, the psychologist William James, who was a very patriotic American democrat, once said of Henry's novels that "they give a certain impression of the author clinging to his gentlemanliness though all else be lost, and dying happy provided it be *sans déroger*."

Even if this judgment is true—even, that is, if there is a streak of finicky gentlemanliness in Henry James—it is beside the point. The idea that James wrote as he did because he was snobbish and that his novels are boring because they fail to describe wars, acts of sexual violence, or sweating poker players is about as reasonable as the idea that Jane Austen's novels are trivial because she wrote exclusively about the country gentry of her time and nowhere describes a lusty seduction or the Napoleonic wars.

It is true that James did little to placate his audience's prejudices against gentlemanliness. Nothing is more American about him than the completeness, even extravagance, with which he committed himself to his chosen subject and manner. This much at least he had in common with Mark Twain, who committed himself with similar completeness to life on the Mississippi. The difference between them is that the subject Twain chose, or perhaps was chosen by, and the personality it imposed on him were just the ones to appeal to a wide audience, whereas the ones James chose were anathema to that audience. Yet that difference was not in the long run altogether an advantage to Twain. All his books were immense popular successes, but only two of them—*Huckleberry Finn* and *Life on the Mississippi*—are great books, and even they are flawed in a way that makes their greatness seem almost an accident. None of Henry James's novels was a great popular success and perhaps none of them ever will be, but at least half a dozen of them are great novels. It is as easy to dislike James for irrelevant reasons as it is to like Mark Twain, but the rewards of subduing such prejudices as James may at first arouse, until the reader sees how much life he can communicate by describing his cultivated ladies and gentlemen and how much awareness he can express in his elaborate manner, are very great.

James's gentlemanlines was quite natural, if not—as his brother's rejection of it shows—inevitable. James was, to be sure, the grandson of a tough and energetic Irish immigrant who made a fortune of three million dollars, but—as Henry himself noticed with amusement—after that "the rupture with my grandfather's tradition and attitude was complete; we were never, in a single case, I think, for two generations, guilty of a stroke of business." Henry's father was a remarkable and attractive man, a close friend of Emerson and Carlyle, an unorthodox but intensely serious transcendentalist, and an idealistic American democrat. He was also intellectually tough, witty, and sardonic, and wholly incapable of what he called "the flagrant morality" common in his time. He had earned his unorthodox religious convictions by living through a serious spiritual crisis—known in the family with typical Jamesian comic precision as a "vastation"—and he never forgot its lesson. "Every man who has reached his intellectual teens," he said, "begins to suspect . . . that [life] flowers and fructifies . . . out of the profoundest tragic depths,—the depths of the essential dearth in which its subject's roots are plunged. . . . The natural inheritance of everyone who is capable of spiritual life is an unsubdued forest where the wolf howls and the obscene bird of night chatters." That sentence could have been written by his son Henry.

The life of the James family—there were five talented children—was a venture in American idealism, a thoroughgoing experiment—made possible by the James's wealth—with the democratic idea that everyone ought to be free to develop his own gifts, unrestrained by conventional habits of any kind. The family moved restlessly from place to place, so that the children were never absorbed into any community, and it was an established practice with the elder James to move them from one school to another to minimize the dangers of formal education. In order to assure himself that there would be no loafing on the job, he also encouraged complete freedom of discussion within the family circle, where the hitting out in argument, if always affectionate, was often extremely rough. The social consequence of this was that the children were aliens everywhere except within the family, which was very close indeed· because it had to provide everything a society usually provides as well as what a family does, and all the children grew up to be citizens of no country except what William once called the James country.

It was a heavy strain on them and did considerable damage; two of the James boys failed miserably ever to find their way in the world and the one girl in the family, Alice, despite her great natural abilities, was almost completely incapacitated for most of her life by nervous disorders. But both Henry and William, after serious crises, survived as triumphant if eccentric illustrations of the virtues of this upbringing.

One of its strangest consequences was that Henry developed a passion for the orderly, cultivated, conventional life of the upper classes, almost as if, having grown up in the cold, he could never again endure anything but the hottest of houses. Thirty-odd years before his death he moved permanently to England, and the older he grew, the more elaborately formal his manners became, both in his life and in his books. But he was never at home in this world in the way one born and raised in it would be, and he always felt like an immigrant. Late in his life, in a moment of depression, he said to a visitor, "the mixture of Europe and America which you see in me has proved disastrous. . . . I have lost touch with my own people, and live here alone." But if living so was painful, it nevertheless allowed James to see, as only an outsider can, the shortcomings and absurdities of the society hé had made himself a part of, and in all James's anxious and often extravagantly literal performances of the manners of his adopted society, whether in his personal life or in his books, there is an element of irony, sometimes amused and sometimes grim.

This irony is always ready to pounce when James is describing the life of the English upper class to which he had committed himself, as is the complementary irony he reserved for the provincial rigidity of the Americans in his novels whose idealistic individualism he so much respected. The complementary insights that made these two kinds of irony posible for James were the rewards of the painful mixture within him of Europe and America, and their importance cannot be exaggerated. The effect of the first is beautifully represented in the little fancy Ford Madox Ford produced in his description of James worrying over the hiring of a "Lady Help" for Lamb House, his establishment at Rye.

> So the poor Master . . . had to spend long mornings and afternoons on what he called "the benches of desolation in purgatorial, if I may allow myself the word, establishments, ill-named, since no one appeared there to register themselves . . . eminently ill-named: *registry-offices* . . ." And there would be a sound like the hiss of a snake as he uttered the compound word. . . .
>
> He would pass his time, he said, interviewing ladies all of a certain age, all of haughty—the French would say *renfrognée*—expressions, all of whom would unanimously assure him that, if they demeaned themselves merely by for an instant considering the idea of entering the household of an untitled person like himself, in such a God-forsaken end of the world as the Ancient Town of Rye, they having passed their lives in the families of never anyone less than a belted earl in mansions on Constitution Hill in the shadow of Buckingham Palace . . . if they for a fleeting moment toyed with the idea, it was merely, they begged to assure him . . . "forthegoodoftheirhealths." Mr. James having dallied with this sentence would utter the last words with extreme rapidity, raising his eyebrows and his cane in the air and digging the ferrule suddenly into the surface of the road. . . .
>
> How they come back to me after a quarter of a century . . . the savoured, half-humorous, half-deprecatory words, the ironically exaggerated gestures, the workings of the closely shaven lips, the halting to emphasize a point, the sudden scurryings forward, for all the world like the White Rabbit hurrying to the Queen's tea-party.

James's serious concern to sustain in his life the ritual of upper-class existence is plain enough there; this was the way of life he had chosen and he meant to make a success of it however much trouble it cost him. At the same time he was, as half an outsider, acutely aware that this ritual was not a part of the divinely ordained nature of things, much as people like the haughty *grandes dames* of the registry offices might think it was, but only the artificial style of a small class. Those long mornings he has spent in registry offices and his irritation, sustained into the present, at the inadequacy of what they had to offer him show his seriousness; at the same time the comic proliferation of qualifying clauses and the deliberate exaggeration of his gestures convey his ironic amusement over the passionate dedication to the rigid customs of upper-class society of its unemployed servants—and of the Henry James who is hiring one of them. Henry James was, in short, the kind of upper-class Englishman that only a relatively classless American—and a very unusual one at that—can be.

The effect of the second kind of irony—of the Europeanized James's awareness of the American's provinciality—can be seen in almost any of his descriptions of ordinary Americans abroad. The hero of *The Ambassadors,* for example, meets in Europe a lifelong New England friend, an immensely successful lawyer named Waymarsh, who is abroad trying to recover from a nervous breakdown. Waymarsh is, in the integrity of his New England ideas, an admirable as well as a comic figure, and later in the novel a cosmopolitan Parisian lady takes him up with enthusiasm, enchanted by his heroic imperviousness to the charms of Parisian life; "so grand is it," she says, "not to understand." When someone else points out that Waymarsh is like "Moses, in the ceiling [of the Sistine Chapel], brought down to the floor; overwhelming, colossal, but somehow portable," Miss Barrace says:

> "Certainly, if you mean by portable, looking so well in one's carriage. . . . he looks like somebody, somebody foreign and famous, *en exile;* so that people wonder—it's very amusing—whom

I am taking about. I show him Paris, show him everything, and he never turns a hair. He's like the Indian chief one reads about, who, when he comes up to Washington to see the Great Father, stands wrapped in his blanket and gives no sign."

This European vision of his old friend makes Strether sad, for he himself has, in his Jamesian sensitivity to Europe, turned all too many hairs and lost the aids to integrity of Waymarsh's blindness. "Strether's sadness," as James says, "sprang—for the image had its grandeur —from his thinking how little he himself was wrapped in his blanket, how little, in marble halls, all too oblivious of the Great Father, he resembled a really majestic aboriginal."

Needless to say, feeling as he does about Europe, Waymarsh has been little helped by European travel. But then James brings him together in Paris with an equally rigid New England lady who has come over to extricate her brother from a love affair with what she is sure is a despicably immoral French woman. And suddenly Paris—or *a* Paris, anyhow, the Paris of the American tourist—becomes dazzling for Waymarsh as he finds himself involved in a comically proper romance with Mrs. Pocock—"dining her, nose to nose, at the hour when all Paris is crowding to profane delights, and in the—well, in the great temple, as one hears of it, of pleasure."

> "That's just *it,* for both of them," Strether insisted—"and all of a supreme innocence. The Parisian place, the feverish hour, the putting before her of a hundred francs' worth of food and drink, which they'll scarcely touch—all that's the dear man's romance; the expensive kind, expensive in francs and centimes, in which he abounds. And the circus afterwards—which is cheaper, but which he'll find some means of making as dear as possible—that's also *his* tribute to the ideal. . . . They won't talk of anything worse than you and me."

James's commitment to upper-class English life was undoubtedly the most important act of his life. It was a commitment to an actual society, and it saved him from the temptation that always lies in wait for the writer who is romantically appealed to by idealism, as the son of a transcendentalist American philosopher could hardly fail to be. This is the temptation to ignore the limits set by the everyday life of organized society on the realization of the idealist's dreams. James observed with remarkable insight and unhesitating honesty the limits set on men's lives in upper-class British society and he fully understood the power it had to prevent anyone's breaking through those limits. He saw that the setting of limits by this society was not a disadvantage unique to it that could be escaped from by destroying that society or running away from it to some other one—"lighting out for the Territory." Similar limits, he could see, were set by every society, and the ones set by his society were merely particular instances of the limits set everywhere by life itself. Seeing this, he scrupulously kept the achievements of his American idealists—however much he sympathized with their ideals—within these limits. As a result both the successes and the defeats of his idealists are wholly convincing because they occur, not in some convenient dream of the world as it ought to be, but in a world we know actually exists and is exemplary of all life.

James's novels are in this sense realistic novels of manners, though their realism is often stretched to the breaking point by his efforts to represent fully the subtle spiritual life of his characters. These efforts drove him to deal with characters so refined in perception and so clever in analysis that some readers refuse to accept them. From a simple statistical point of view their objections are perfectly valid; these characters are no more representative of their class and kind than the exceptional heroes and heroines of great literature ever are. But they are nonetheless believable human beings in a real world, because James knew his society and the people who live in it so well and was so scrupulous in presenting them as they were that we cannot help being convinced by them.

James is thus the first novelist to bring the highly idealizing American imagination, with its obsessive interest in what Hawthorne called "some less obvious peculiarity of the subject . . . than a counterfeit of real life," to terms with the observable reality of actual life that such a counterfeit is designed to present. In the strict sense of the term, he is the first great American *novelist,* as distinguished from writers of allegorical or symbolic romances like Hawthorne and Melville, or writers of pastoral fables like Cooper and Mark Twain.

The typical James novel describes a dramatic clash between a romantic belief in life's limitless possibilities for self-discovery and self-improvement (usually held by an American character, often a woman), and a highly developed sense of the value and the power of society and of the limited possibilities open to the individual (usually felt by a European character). James wanted to explore the psychological, emotional, and moral aspects of this conflict; in order to do so, he wrote about the lives of well-to-do Americans living in Europe, particularly in Paris and London. Such people have the leisure and— at their best—the cultivation to experience the subtle conflicts of feelings and moral attitudes that constitute the drama of James's novels, and in order to show them doing so, James developed a complicated and elaborate prose style that would allow him to "render"—as he called it—every shade of his characters' thoughts and feelings and all the ironies he could see in their situation.

The American hero of the typical James novel is always defeated by the insistence of society on obedience to its own customs, which he feels have little to do with what he cares for and are often invoked in selfish and even brutal ways. But he cannot escape these customs; they are in effect the conditions of existence itself and therefore, taken in the right way, the occasions of true heroism. From the beginning to the end of James's career his novels make this point. In one of his first major works, *The American* (1876), the hero voluntarily passes up a chance to revenge himself on the aristocratic French family that has betrayed him because it cannot, when it comes right down to it, bear to have its daughter make an unconventional marriage with a barbarous American. In one of the last, *The Ambassadors* (1903), the hero defies the customs of his own New England society at considerable cost to himself in an unsuccessful effort to assist the French

heroine and then refuses to accept even the smallest return for having
done so. The greatness of James's heroes is the magnanimity with
which they accept the defeats by conventional society of their efforts
to realize their ideals.

All this can best be seen in the novel James himself thought his
finest, *The Ambassadors*. *The Ambassadors* sets forth the typical
James story of the intelligent but provincial American who, confronted by the richness and complexity of European life, rises trium-
phantly to the occasion for understanding it offers him, without losing
the almost Puritan firmness of his highly refined New England conscience. It is Lambert Strether's appreciation of the wide range of new
possibilities opened up to him by Europe that allows him to see the
beauty of its "immoral" life; it is his American idealism that leads
him to risk—and eventually sacrifice—his own future in a losing effort to save the novel's Parisian heroine; it is the integrity of his New
England conscience, transformed but not weakened by his understanding of Europe, that makes him refuse to profit in any way from
what he has done.

The ambassadors of the novel's title are emissaries sent by the great
lady of a New England town, Woollett, Massachusetts, to Paris to
rescue her son from the clutches of what everyone in Woollett assumes
without question is a wicked and vulgar French woman. This son,
Chad Newsome, has been lingering in Paris in a scandalously friv-
olous way when he should have come home to take his proper place
in the family business now that his father is dead. Lambert Strether
is the first ambassador Mrs. Newsome sends. He has long been a close
friend of the family and has lately arrived at one of those queer, un-
spoken, New England understandings with the widowed Mrs. Newsome; they are in effect engaged, and Strether therefore comes to
Paris in an almost paternal capacity to rescue Chad. He also comes,
however, as a man who has always been aware of the provinciality of
New England life and felt a longing for the greater range of Europe.
His purpose in coming to Paris is therefore twofold. He is to rescue
Chad and bring him home to the business in Woollett for Mrs. New-

some—a beautifully comic New England version of the dangerous adventure undertaken by the gallant knight in order to win his lady's hand. He is at the same time, for himself, to experience something of the beauty and splendor of European life.

The novel opens with Strether arriving at Liverpool, intent on his mission to rescue Chad and confident in the belief that Chad's life in Europe is vulgarly immoral. But he is, as James says, "burdened, poor Strether—it had better be confessed at the outset—with the oddity of a double consciousness. There was detachment in his zeal and curiosity in his indifference," and he finds himself delaying his journey to Chester, where he is to meet Waymarsh, and wandering about even so dull a town as Liverpool with delight. When he does reach Chester, he falls in with a thoroughly Europeanized American woman named Maria Gostrey even before he can get in touch with Waymarsh.

These three take a long walk around Chester, and, to Waymarsh's distress and Miss Gostrey's delight, Strether responds to its charms with enthusiasm. Suddenly Waymarsh dashes across the street into a jeweler's shop, and Strether and Miss Gostrey discuss why he has done so in one of James's brilliant, elliptical, penetrating passages of dialogue, the very understanding of which on Strether's part is, as it is part of his fault to be able to see, a kind of betrayal. " 'I've known you a few hours,' he says to Miss Gostrey, 'and I've known *him* all my life; so that if the ease I thus take with you about him isn't magnificent'—and the thought of it held him a moment—'why, it's rather base.' "

What Strether and Miss Gostrey make out between them is that Waymarsh is defying European values. When Miss Gostrey says to Strether, "What's the matter with him?" Strether says, "Well, he can't stand it"; and when Miss Gostrey asks him what Waymarsh can't stand, Strether says, "Anything. Europe." He quickly realizes that Waymarsh's American way of asserting his freedom may be to buy out the whole shop. When Waymarsh returns without giving an indication of what he has done—it is his distinction never to do so—Miss

Gostrey says, "I am convinced he has been splendid, and has been
so for you," but Strether says,

> "Ah, no—not that."
> "Then for me?"
> "Quite as little."
> "Then for himself?"
> "For nobody. For nothing. For freedom."
> "But what has freedom to do with it?"
> Strether's answer was indirect. "To be as good as you and me.
> But different."

Watching Strether's face closely and seeing all he really is, Miss Gostrey then sums up James's essential point about Strether. "Different,"
she says, "—yes. But better!"

With such fine discriminations of the meanings of his characters'
situations and conduct, James carries Strether to Paris. There he finally catches up with Chad, only to discover that the awkward and
insensitive boy he had known in Woollett has become a handsome
and cultivated man who seems to know everyone worth knowing in
Paris and is easily at home everywhere. It gives him an uncomfortable
feeling that Paris has not been so bad for Chad as they had all assumed back in Woollett, and this feeling is reinforced by the way
Strether himself has been moved by its beauty. James makes us feel
what Paris means to Strether at every turn, as for example when he
sees the house of a great artist to which Chad takes him.

> Far back from the street and unsuspected by crowds, reached by a
> long passage and a quiet court, it was as striking to the unprepared
> mind, he immediately saw, as a treasure dug up; giving him too,
> more than anything yet, the note of the range of the immeasurable
> town and sweeping away, as by a last brave brush, his usual land-
> marks and terms. It was in the garden, a spacious, cherished rem-
> nant, that Chad's host presently met them; while the tall bird-
> haunted trees, all of a twitter with the spring and the weather, and
> the high party-walls, on the other side of which grave *hôtels* stood
> off for privacy, spoke of survival, transmission, association, a

strong, indifferent, persistent order. The day was so soft that the little party had practically adjourned to the open air, but the open air, in such conditions, was all a chamber of state.

Then it gradually dawns on Strether that the miraculous transformation of Chad can only have been the work of some sensitive and highly civilized woman; and sure enough he presently meets a quietly distinguished lady of great charm and beauty who is evidently in some way closely involved with Chad. Far from being the wicked and vulgar French woman of Woollett's imagination, she is so marvelous that Strether goes through a tortured series of tragi-comic maneuvers in order to allow himself to believe that the relation between Chad and Mme. de Vionnet is what he calls "a virtuous attachment." He first persuades himself that Chad is in love with Mme. de Vionnet's daughter. But this theory does not survive his discovery that Chad has helped Mme. de Vionnet to arrange, in the best French style, a highly desirable marriage of convenience for her daughter. He then resorts to an almost pitifully New England romantic vision of their relation. "I understand," he says, "what a relation with such a woman—what such a high, fine friendship—may be. It can't be vulgar or coarse, anyway—and that's the point." Strether of course means by "vulgar or coarse" sexual, a literal love affair. The friend to whom he is speaking, knowing the truth about Chad and Mme. de Vionnet, can nonetheless assent to Strether's description, for he knows that, however otherwise wrong Strether may be, he is not wrong in thinking their relation is not vulgar or coarse—not wrong in thinking that it is, perhaps in a better sense than he knows, a virtuous attachment—anyway on Mme. de Vionnet's part.

Meanwhile, during the long delays occasioned by Strether's working out his assessment of the new Chad and his situation, the formidable Mrs. Newsome has been growing more and more impatient of Strether's incomprehensible failure to bring Chad back to Woollett. Gradually she has ceased even to answer the letters in which Strether more and more despairingly seeks to explain to her the fineness of Chad's life in Paris and the way his understanding of it has changed his determination to bring Chad home. Finally she acts. New ambassadors are sent out to Paris—Mrs. Newsome's daughter, Sarah Pocock, her husband, and his sister, an attractive young American girl that Woollett, despite all its ostensible disapproval of the powers of sex, has coldly calculated will catch Chad for them. It is one of James's characteristic ironies that this girl turns out to be one of those Americans who sees the splendor of Europe, and she sides with Strether rather than with Mrs. Pocock.

But Sarah Pocock is all Newsome, fierce in her provincial New England moralism, wholly insensitive to Europe, and brutally determined to have her own way. She tells Strether he is sacrificing Mrs. Newsome out of some kind of infatuation with "that woman," as she calls Mme. de Vionnet. But Strether is as determined to live by the values of his new sense of life as Sarah is to live by the values of the old one. He therefore uses all the influence he has on Chad, in direct opposition to Mrs. Pocock, to keep Chad in Paris, thus sacrificing his last hope of marrying Mrs. Newsome and gaining for himself the comfort and companionship of a secure life in Woollett.

It is just at this point, when he has burned all his bridges behind him, that Strether discovers the relation between Chad and Mme. de Vionnet is not—in his sense of the term—a virtuous attachment at all but a passionate love affair. This is a terrible blow to a man of his New England upbringing, but James shows us the kind of moral heroism possessed by what he liked to call "my poor gentleman" by having Strether finally recognize that only by loving Chad in this way, completely, could Mme. de Vionnet have transformed him as she has. Seeing Mme. de Vionnet's love in its full human reality, undeluded any longer by the provincial assurances of Woollett, Strether also begins to discriminate between her love for Chad and Chad's for her, to see that, for all Chad's improvement, he is still fundamentally a Newsome; this fact is made undeniably clear when Chad starts to show signs of thinking it would be rather fun to go home and run the business and make a lot of money.

Thus, by a grand ironic reversal, Strether now sees Mme. de Vionnet—that wicked and vulgar French woman of Woollett's fantasy of life—as the only person in the story who has acted with perfect purity of heart, for he now knows how deep and desperate her love for Chad is. There is a magnificent moment when, knowing all this, and knowing too that Mme. de Vionnet is aware that he does, Strether goes to call on her.

It was of Chad [he saw, that] she was, after all, renewedly afraid; the strange strength of her passion was the very strength of her fear. . . . With this sharpest perception yet, it was like a chill in the air to him, it was almost appalling, that a creature so fine could be, by mysterious forces, a creature so exploited. . . . He presently found himself taking a long look from her, and the next thing he knew he had uttered all his thought. "You're afraid for your life!"

A spasm came into her face, the tears she had already been unable to hide overflowed first in silence, and then, as the sound suddenly comes from a child, quickened to gasps, to sobs. . . . "It's how you see me, it's how you see me"—she caught her breath with it—"and it's as I *am,* and as I must take myself, and of course it's no matter." . . . He couldn't say it was not no matter; for he was serving her to the end, he now knew, anyway— quite as if what he thought of her had nothing to do with it. It was actually moreover as if he didn't think of her at all, as if he could think of nothing but the passion, mature, abysmal, pitiful, she represented, and the possibilities she betrayed. She was older for him tonight, visibly less exempt from the touch of time; but she was as much as ever the finest and subtlest creature, the happiest apparition, it had been given him, in all his years, to meet; and yet he could see her there as vulgarly troubled, in very truth, as a maidservant crying for her young man.

It is because Strether is so deeply moved by Mme. de Vionnet's fineness and by the terrible humiliation her love for Chad has put on her that he suddenly knows he is going to serve her to the end. Characteristically he immediately offers her any help in his power. This generosity reminds her in turn of how much she has come to admire

F

Strether and how bitterly she hates having, as she believes, lost his
respect by what she has done to hold Chad. "You don't care," she
says, "what I think of you; but I happen to care what you think of
me." Strether can only say, "You're wonderful."

> "I'm old and abject and hideous"—she went on as without hear-
> ing him. "Abject above all. Or old above all. It's when one's old
> that it's the worst. It's a doom—I know it; you can't see it more
> than I do myself. Things have to happen as they will." With which
> she came back to what, face to face with him, had so quite broken
> down. "Of course you wouldn't, even if possible, and no matter
> what happened, be near [me]. But think of me, think of me—!"

It is a terrible moment, for us as well as for Strether. This proud and
beautiful woman, refined in a way Strether has never known before
by the long discipline of her class and tradition, has been driven by
her uncontrollable passion to do what she hates so much that she believes Strether cannot endure the sight of her; and now she is reduced
to pleading for his sympathy.

Even worse, both Strether and Mme. de Vionnet know that whatever Chad may say, he is at bottom too much a Newsome, too much
an American like Waymarsh, not ultimately to grow tired of the cul-
tured leisure of Paris and to yearn irresistibly for the business world
of Woollett. For all Newsomes, Europe, whether they like it or not,
is simply entertainment, not life; and Chad's affair with Mme. de
Vionnet, for all the superior knowledge of life Mme. de Vionnet has
been able to give it, is for Chad only a more sophisticated version of
the little Parisian romance between Sarah Pocock and Waymarsh.

Of all the ambassadors from Woollett, only Strether has fully understood that Europe at its best, as he has seen it in Paris, is life lived
at a depth and with a beauty that is unknown elsewhere, and he sees
Mme. de Vionnet as the quintessence of this life. In a sense he understands this better than any European does, because he has brought
to his experience of Europe his American capacity for wonder, his
responsiveness to the extraordinary possibilities for an ideal life that

Europe opens up. Not that he can bring about the fulfillment of these possibilities; the unbreachable conditioning of all the other participants in the affair except Mme. de Vionnet by the customs of their society makes that impossible. Nonetheless Strether goes down fighting, true to the end to the vision of the ideal life that he has long since seen is doomed to defeat. It is a triumph of the New England integrity of conscience that he has now learned to use with perfected insight. How doomed to defeat he is has been all too evident to him during his last meeting with Chad, when Chad "had thrown back his light overcoat and thrust each of his thumbs into the armhole of his waistcoat; in which position his fingers played up and down." In this revealing pose, Chad launches into an enthusiastic account of the extraordinary effects of advertising, which he describes "as an art like another, and infinitely like all the arts." Strether could only watch him helplessly "quite as if, there on the pavement, without a pretext, he had begun to dance a fancy step." Chad also assures him that he "is not a bit tired" of Mme. de Vionnet. "He meant no harm," Strether thinks, "though he might after all be capable of much; yet he spoke of being 'tired' of her almost as he might have spoken of being tired of roast mutton for dinner."

In the novel's first scene, Maria Gostrey had told Strether that part of what had immediately attracted her to him was that he was a failure. "Look about you," she had said, "—look at the successes. Would you *be* one, on your honor?" And then, with a touch of feminine ego that reveals there is something more in her feelings for Strether than interest in his intelligence, she adds, "Look, moreover, at me." After he has done so for a moment, Strether says, "I see. You too are out of it." "The superiority you discern in me," she says ironically, "announces my futility." "If you knew," she adds, as if to enforce the resemblance between them, "the dreams of my youth!" Then, as if to warn him of his fate, she says, "But our *realities* are what has brought us together. We're beaten brothers in arms."

Logically enough, then, in the last scene of the novel, Maria Gostrey, with a quiet unconventionality perfectly characteristic of James's

ostensibly "eviscerated" characters, flatly proposes to Strether.
"There's nothing, you know, I wouldn't do for you," she says. "I
know. I know," Strether answers. "But all the same I must go. To be
right." With an almost desperate pretense that she doesn't understand
him, Miss Gostrey says, "To be right?" But, as James says, Strether
"felt it already clear for her"; nonetheless he makes it quite explicit.
"That, you see, is my only logic. Not, out of the whole affair, to have
got anything for myself." Once more Miss Gostrey tries to dodge the
truth she clearly understands: "But with your wonderful impressions,
you'll have got a great deal." But Strether will not let her dodge: "A
great deal," he agrees. "But nothing like *you*. It's you who would
make me wrong!"

And then, at last, she gives in. "It isn't so much your *being* 'right',"
she says with a mock bitterness that is in fact only a pretense of mock-
ery, "—it's your horrible sharp eye for what makes you so." But it
is, of course—this is James's whole point about those who possess
both the American's idealistic integrity of purpose and the European's
full understanding of life—both. Strether answers her complaint
against him by reminding her that they are, indeed, however badly
their different hopes may be defeated, "beaten brothers in arms." "Oh,
but you're just as bad yourself," he says. "You can't resist me when
I point that out." It leaves Miss Gostrey helpless. It is true that she
loves him because he has the integrity to act rightly and the insight
to know how to; at the same time, it is precisely his insight and his
integrity that are making him refuse her. She sums up everything she
feels about this dilemma in a wry variation on Strether's words: "I
can't indeed," she says, "resist you." And Strether brings the whole
story to a conclusion by saying, "Then, there we are!" His point is
not only that they both understand exactly where they and all the rest
of the characters in the novel have ended up; it is also that they know
they have to accept all that that means, know that things have to be
as they are. It is as much as to say that there, if we have really read
The Ambassadors, we as readers are too, understanding and accepting as unavoidable the fate of everyone in the novel. James's novels

may be—indeed they are—novels of manners, comedies in the old, full sense of the word. But his "poor gentlemen" come as close as any figures of American fiction to being the tragic heroes of modern Western culture.

EDITH WHARTON
1862-1937

The Age of Innocence
1923

Edith Wharton is an unusual kind of novelist for American literature
to have produced. The exceptional circumstances of her upbringing
gave her insights and created conflicts for her not very common
among American novelists, and gave her a mastery of material rarely
available to them. Her good friend, Henry James, was also born into
the New York social world Edith Wharton grew up in, though at a
slightly earlier time. But James did not know that world as she did:
his father was so unusual a man that the James children hardly grew
up in any social world. Edith Wharton had the proud sense of privacy
of her class, no doubt intensified by the lifelong shyness that was an
open agony to her as a child and perhaps no less an agony to her as
an adult, however well she had learned to cover it up.

As a consequence she never discussed the conflicts in her life or
the complicated tensions of feelings they generated within her, though
it is perhaps some measure of how severe these tensions were—and
their queer mixture of intellectual ambition and yearning for an impossibly perfect lover—that she seems all her life to have half-believed
her brothers' "extremely cultivated English tutor" was her real father. By a kind of mortmain she succeeded in imposing her own dis-

cretion on the friends who have been responsible, since her death, for our knowledge of her life, and there has been an unfortunate and surely unnecessary amount of mystification about the sources of her work in her personal experience. The result has been an unsympathetic conception of her character and a confusion between the work that expresses her whole nature and her merely clever and skillful work, of which she produced an unusual amount.

Recently scholars like Wayne Andrews and Millicent Bell have cleared up a good deal of the mystery about Mrs. Wharton, and it is possible now to understand her reasonably well; no doubt we shall learn a good many more interesting facts about her life, but it seems reasonable to suppose that the main outlines of her character and experience are now clear to us and will not be greatly changed by further information. But this understanding of her has emerged piecemeal, so that what Grace Kellogg has called "the two lives of Edith Wharton" are not even yet widely known, and the effect of understanding them on our conception of her work has scarcely been considered. When Irving Howe recently put together a collection of essays about her work, the best criticism he could find was that of E. K. Brown, now over thirty years old, and that of Blake Nevius, also written before the new knowledge about her had become available.

As a result of these difficulties the critical judgments of her work made in her own day, blurred though they were by the fashions of the time and an unavoidable lack of critical distance, still largely determine the general view of it. There is real injustice to her in this. For one thing, Edith Wharton's deepest feelings were heavily influenced by the world she grew up in, despite her rebellion against that world; but in her own day the life of that world was resented by the intellectual community, so that it tended to overrate the work written by the rebellious Edith Wharton and to describe as sentimental and nostalgic work that showed any sympathy for the world she grew up in, especially as the work of the rebellious Edith Wharton is heavily infected with the views fashionable in the intellectual community of her time, to which she was as anxious in her way to gain an entrée as the

nouveaux riches of her social satires are to make their way in the old
New York society she had grown up in.

Grace Kellogg is certainly right that Edith Wharton lived two distinct—though overlapping—lives; it is equally important to recognize
that she wrote two distinct kinds of books. One kind is the work of
the talented, self-made intellectual (she always remembered with
pride someone's observation that she was "a self-made man"). In
their slightly different ways, such books as *The Fruit of the Tree,
The Custom of the Country,* and *Ethan Frome* are the work of this
Edith Wharton. "I take to her very kindly," Henry James said with
his terrible precision of her early work, "as regards her diabolical
little cleverness, the quantity of intention and intelligence in her style
and her sharp eye for an interesting subject. . . ." But there was another Edith Wharton who dominates books like *The House of Mirth*
for long stretches and *The Age of Innocence* almost completely. This
second Edith Wharton was very nearly a great novelist, and *The Age
of Innocence* is an achievement of a quite different order from the
books written by Edith Wharton the intellectual.

Edith Wharton the intellectual was anxious to understand life in
the best modern way and had a passion for views. As Paul Bourget
said after he had met her, "She has ordered her intellect somewhere,
as we would order a piece of furniture, to measure"; and like some
Undine Spragg of the intelligentsia, she selected this furniture according to a superior but standardized taste in intellectual interior decoration. Bourget concluded that such a woman must be a "thinking machine," but that is almost certainly unjust. Edith Wharton evidently
had some notion that the knowledge and taste she was acquiring were
an extension of her sensibility and an enrichment of her emotional
life, just as she mistook the sterile intellectualism of Walter Berry for
imagination and generosity. She went after both with a self-centered
and almost childlike optimism that was all her life to underlie the
formidably informed upper-class lady she made herself into. There is
something appealing about the passionate if mistaken determination
with which she pursued, confident that it was the way to fulfill her

nature, a mode of life almost perfectly calculated to disappoint those intense feelings she supposed it would satisfy. If Mr. Eliot is right that Edith Wharton's friend Henry James was saved by having a mind too fine to be violated by an idea, then Edith Wharton courted damnation with touching energy.

She was proud of her trained capacity for making a well-wrought desert of up-to-date views and calling it life. Yet, as with many of the intellectual woman like her both before and especially since her time, there was beneath the hard-earned intellectual superiority she achieved some feeling of defeat, some sense of having become formidable and refined in a slightly desiccated way rather than—as she had intended —a woman like the Ellen Olenska of *The Age of Innocence,* whose cultivation is an unselfconscious development of her whole self. A part of Edith Wharton understood all too well that the ludicrous displacement of an attitude by its sign that always marks the *nouveaux riches* in her novels (those ladies who lie in their pink velvet beds with Honiton sheets and cry their eyes out because they are not asked to the musicals of cultivated New York society) was echoed more subtly by New York society itself, with its rigid adherence to customs that had long since lost such value—the understanding of at least Fitzgreen Halleck and the poet of "The Culprit Fay"—as they had once had. This part of Edith Wharton was quite capable of seeing that her own intellectualism was a substitution of opinions for awareness. Perhaps, then, she understood—without always being able to do anything about it—that the energetic collection of antiques and ideas and intellectual duchesses was a confusion of ends and means. She certainly knew that "the soul of the novel . . . is (or should be) the writer's soul," and in the best of her work it is. But this commandment is easier to express than to follow. Anyhow, her devoted friend, Henry James, knew that collecting was accurst, though he also understood his own opposed tendency to worry unnecessarily about an addiction to it. The play of these feelings in the friendship of Edith Wharton and James could be very amusing, perhaps to them as well as to us. There is a chapter in Percy Lubbock's *Portrait of Edith Wharton* describing how she would direct what James called her "urgent and terrible signals" on Lamb House and, almost before James could prepare one of his opulently phrased welcomes for her, would whirl him away on some cultural expedition. James's worry about her restless pursuit of such things, though touched with the humorous acknowledgment of his own opposite weakness, was quite real. "I cannot help regretting," as he said, ". . . that an *intellectuelle*—and an Angel—should require such a big pecuniary basis. How much more consistently intellectual and angelic are *we* in our unmoneyed state."

The undeveloped selves that go on existing beneath the shiny intellectual surfaces of women like Mrs. Wharton take a meaner revenge on them than a restless search for culture, too. What that revenge is can be seen very clearly in the life of George Eliot, an early and more open example of the type, whom Mrs. Wharton greatly admired. George Eliot combined what one of her ill-chosen early lovers, John Chapman, called a "formal and studied" intellectual personality with an uncultivated and yet uncontrollable need to be loved. As a consequence she led an irregular sexual life that had about it a sad air of improvisation. Even sadder—because she was too intelligent not to recognize her own mistakes after making them and sooner or later ascribed them to her heroines—was her tendency to act out with scornful unconventionality her schoolgirl daydreams of romance whenever she fell in with men prepared to use their intellectual prestige to encourage her uncritical adoration. In the most unfortunate way possible, she managed to convince herself that the demands of her second self were simply an expression of her eagerness for culture and to rationalize her indiscretions as the intellectual woman's sensible disregard for stupid conventions.

In 1843 (she was twenty-four) George Eliot was flattered by the recognition of her intellectual powers by a certain Dr. Brabant, "a pompous and rather foolish" man of sixty-two. He invited her to visit him "to fill the place of his daughter." Despite the warnings of well-meaning but not very intellectual friends, she did so, and "knelt at his feet and offered to devote her life to his service," as Eliza Linton put it. "In the simplicity of her heart and her ignorance of (or incapability of practicing) the required conventionalisms, [she] gave the Doctor the utmost attention; they became very intimate." In the end Mrs. Brabant issued an ultimatum, the doctor took fright, and, in what John Chapman called an "unmanly" way, assisted Mrs. Brabant in driving George Eliot from the house. She was almost certainly recalling this episode when she later created the nearly unbearable idealistic foolishness of Dorothea Brooke's marriage with Mr. Casaubon in *Middlemarch:* when a friend asked her where she had got Mr. Casaubon, "with humorous solemnity, which was quite in earnest, she pointed to her own heart."

Edith Wharton was a lady, in a time when a lady's scope for this kind of foolishness was not large. Nevertheless she managed to manifest this characteristic of the type clearly enough; she had her long moment of foolishness with Walter Berry. Walter Berry was an able and intelligent man; he was also a mean and ungenerous one—"dry and narrow and supercilious," as Percy Lubbock says. But Edith Wharton very early succeeded in convincing herself that he was both wise and lovable; she clung to this view despite the accumulation of evidence to the contrary that ended with his failing to marry her after her divorce from Edward Wharton. This was undoubtedly a severer blow to her (and perhaps a greater embarrassment to Berry) than it might otherwise have been because, in her headlong way, Edith Wharton apparently never seriously suspected until too late that the decision as to whether they would marry was not entirely hers to make. The pressure on her to believe it was must have been very great; "Ah, the poverty, the miserable poverty," she said to Charles Du Bos in a rare moment of self-revelation, "of any love outside marriage, of any love that is not a living together, a sharing of all!"

After the failure of her debut in New York society—perhaps as much her mother's fault as the result of her own awkward combination of shyness and scorn—Pussy Jones had fallen in with the young married set in which Walter Berry was an established bachelor with a certain reputation for wickedness. She was, at twenty, a very pretty

girl and they were soon getting themselves talked about. But at some
point Edith's courage for indiscretion seems to have frightened Berry;
he left New York and it was not until a dozen years later, some time
after her marriage to Edward Wharton, that Berry consented to re-
appear to help her and Codman with the writing of *The Decoration
of Houses*. Edith Wharton then had a nervous breakdown; we do not
know its exact character or causes, though it is likely her revived
feelings about Berry were somehow involved. Difficult as her life with
Edward Wharton finally became as he drifted into financial irrespon-
sibility and dissipation, she stood by him—perhaps with an unhelpful
severity beyond her control—until it became hopeless. There is no
evidence that she divorced him for Walter Berry. There is some evidence, however, that the possibility of freedom set her dreaming again
of that ideal mate her foolish heart had made her believe Walter
Berry might be. In the sudden glimpse we get of her private feelings
about Berry in her diary of 1908 (the Whartons were not finally divorced until 1913) we can see the revenge her passionate second self
was taking—the illusions and abasements it imposed on her, and the
shock of its inevitable disappointment.

When you came to dine . . . , you said things that distressed me.
At first it was exquisite. I had my work, and you sat near the
lamp and read me a page of Chevrillon's article in the *Revue de
Paris*. . . . And as I followed you, seeing your mind leap ahead,
as it always does, noting how you instantly single out the finer
values I had missed—discriminated, classified, with that flashing,
illuminating sense of differences and relations that so exquisitely
distinguishes your thought—ah, the illusion I had, of a life in
which such evenings might be a dear, accepted habit! At that moment, indeed, *the lover became her husband*. . . .
Why did you spoil it? Because men and women are different, because—in that respect—and in the way of mental companionship
—what I can give you is so much less interesting, less arresting,
than what I receive from you? . . .
You hurt me—you disillusioned me—and when you left me I
was more deeply yours . . . Ah, the confused processes within us!

This longing to be loved in an impossible way that would satisfy every need of her deprived, importunate heart, a need hardly to be satisfied by any mortal man, least of all a selfish one like Walter Berry, was beyond her control. The diary shows it overcoming her good sense again and again: "We had another dear half-hour, coming back from St. C.—last Sunday: . . . I felt your dearest side then, the side that is simple and sensitive and true . . . and I felt all that must have been, at first, so unintelligible to you in me and my life, was clear at last, and that our hearts *and our minds* met. . . ." It was these moments of irrepressible self-deception that made her disillusionments so bitter to her.

> In the train yesterday I was reading Locke's *Heredity and Variation,* and struck by a curious and rather amusing passage, held it out and said: "Read that!"
> The answer was: "Does that sort of thing really amuse you?"
> —I heard the key turn in the prison lock. That is the answer to everything worth-while!
> Oh, Gods of derision! And you have given me twenty years of it!
> *Je n'en peux plus.*

But she could, because she had to. It was not until it became unavoidably clear that Berry had no intention of letting the lover become the husband that she allowed herself to recognize the truth, and then she tried, as she put it, to "face at once the fact that it is over." But even then she could not control her disintegrating yearning for him: "But oh, my adored, my own love, you who have given me the only moments of real life I have ever known, how am I to face the long hours and days. . . ?" She saw that this passion was destroying the intellectual personality she had constructed for herself. *"Malgré moi,* I am a little humbled, a little ashamed, to find how poor a thing I am, how the personality I had moulded into such strong, firm lines has crumbled to a pinch of ashes in this flame! For the first time in my life *I can't read!* . . . I hold the book in my hand, and see your

name all over the page." This image of what was to her complete
demoralization—not being able to read—is grotesquely convincing,
at once absurd and pitiful.

Yet, though she understood what was happening to her, she could
not prevent herself from writing just at this time (between 1908 and
her divorce in 1913) *The Reef,* that beautifully made Jamesian novel
that is so pathetic a revelation of her dream. *The Reef* begins with a
casual affair of its hero, George Darrow; this affair is a sort of accident, about which George Darrow feels embarrassed rather than—
as it is hard not to imagine Walter Berry feeling about his affairs—
pleased: it is Edith Wharton's way of exorcizing the carefully conducted wickednesses of Walter Berry's life. The novel then focuses on
the heroine, Anna Leath. Anna Leath lives so completely in her
dream of an ideal emotional life—and her author lives in that dream
too—that one cannot imagine her ever coming to terms with a world
not wholly dictated by that dream or with a man not impossibly gifted
in anticipating her emotional demands and impossibly devoted to
meeting them. Mrs. Wharton solves this difficulty by making George
Darrow something very like that impossible man, thus giving Anna
Leath's dream the fulfillment Edith Wharton could not, even under
the best of circumstances, have known in reality. It took Mrs. Wharton a dozen years to transmute this wish-fulfilling daydream into the
mature attitude of *The Age of Innocence.*

The difficulties of self-made intellectual women like George Eliot
and Edith Wharton make one think, by contrast, of women writers
like Jane Austen. For all her intelligence, Jane Austen was certainly
not an intellectual, a deprivation that it is fashionable today to pity
her for; but that deprivation seems never to have bothered her. She
lived her quiet life far from the intellectual society of London, and
even when she was in London seems to have been more interested in
inventing jokes for her family about her search for the portrait of
Elizabeth Mr. Darcy must have commissioned after their marriage
than in participating in the life of the fashionable intellectual world.
It is apparently the simple truth that, as she said, "Three or four fam-

ilies in a country village [are] the delight of my life." Perhaps it was a consequence of that mode of life that her passions were so strongly colored by her intelligence. No doubt she found the possibilities for Elizabeth Bennet and Emma Woodhouse in her own heart, but she never found the behavior of these heroines in the conduct of her own life. On the contrary, the little we know about the conduct of her life suggests that it was the author of her novels and not their heroines who controlled it. At least she met the death of that young man from Devonshire who her sister Cassandra plainly implies was the one real love of her life with the same quiet self-control with which she rejected the thoroughly respectable Harrison Bigg-Withers, whom she did not love.

But if the intellectual self Edith Wharton worked with such eager earnestness to create left out of account an important and in the end irrepressible part of her nature, that intellectual self was no small achievement. "You may find her difficult," as James put it, "but you will never find her stupid, and you will never find her mean." This Edith Wharton was of her kind a very able writer, whose limitations are evident to us mainly because, at least once, she managed to get her whole self into a book and show us what she was capable of when she was not writing to satisfy merely her intellectual self. It is impossible, for example, not to respect *The Custom of the Country,* the intellectual Edith Wharton's telling comment on the fashionable problem of the socially ambitious New Woman of American society in her time; it has a harsh, even arrogant, satiric power that is very impressive, and the wealth of relevant social observation and of revealing particulars of dress, of furniture, of customs with which she surrounds the life of her beautiful and naïvely ambitious middle-western heroine, Undine Spragg, is astonishing.

The failure of *The Custom of the Country*—if it is fair to call it a failure in any sense—is its failure to be something different and better than Edith Wharton chose to make it. Henry James was suggesting to her what it might have been when he wrote her, in his circuitously critical way, "But of course you know—as how should you, with your infernal keenness of perception, *not know*—that in doing your tale you had under your hand a magnificent subject ["a crude young woman such as Undine Spragg entering, all unprepared and unperceiving, into the mysterious labyrinth of family life in the old French aristocracy" by marrying Raymond de Chelles], which ought to have been your main theme, and that you used as a mere incident and then passed it by?" The treatment of Undine's French marriage is, in fact, nearly perfect for the kind of book Mrs. Wharton chose to write, a picaresque social satire. But we can see what James was driving at if we look at her much fuller treatment of Undine's second marriage, to Ralph Marvell. By fixing our attention for long periods on Ralph and his tragedy, this treatment distracts our attention from the book's central purpose, its satiric account of Undine Spragg's life, and it is in this sense a fault. Yet in itself this episode is the best thing in the book, a product of something like the full powers of Mrs. Wharton's imagination, not merely of her satiric intellect. In a different way a book like *Ethan Frome* also shows the limiting effect of her commitment to her intellectual self. It too is, in its way, an impressive book, but it is impressive rather as an act of the will than of the imagination. It is a deliberate adoption of an attitude and an image not natural to Mrs. Wharton's understanding; in roundabout ways she does manage to get constricted expressions of some of her deepest feelings into it, but it is essentially a brilliantly performed pastiche. Many of her short stories like "Roman Fever" have a similar character; they are entertaining in the best sense—precisely thought-out, wittily, almost epigrammatically expressed, extremely well made; but there is very little felt life in them.

In her best work, however, in a novel like *The Age of Innocence,* she is a great deal more than just an impressively clever writer; *The Age of Innocence* is very nearly a great novel, though it would be no service to it to pretend that it is some kind of miracle wholly without evidence of the limitations so prominent in Mrs. Wharton's other work. Her impulse to illustrate her views instead of to represent meaningful experience occasionally appears in it, though never in a way to damage it seriously. It is only an annoyance when she cannot resist the temptation to let a series of accidents send Newland Archer and May Welland to spend their honeymoon in the patroon's house on the van der Luyden's estate, where Newland had first recognized, too late, that he loved Ellen Olenska; or that at the crisis of Newland's frustration by his stiflingly conventional marriage, she should have him throw open the library window (on "reality" of course) and announce portentously that "I shall never be happy unless I can open windows." The worst of these displays of cleverness is perhaps the way she has May tear her wedding dress when Newland is longing to run off with Ellen. May's wearing her wedding dress to the opera that night because she believes she is pregnant is at once a fine expression of her character and a gesture that focuses a good many of the novel's conflicting attitudes. But her tearing its hem as she and Newland arrive home is, even as an accident, wholly unlike her, and Mrs. Wharton forces this accident onto the action in order to create a crude and even sentimental symbol for the novel's feelings about Newland's marriage.

Once or twice, too, she forces her material irresponsibly to make mere social comments, as when she presses the contrast between Fanny Beaufort, the illegitimate daughter of the novel's unscrupulous financier whom Newland Archer's son marries, and Ellen Olenska, whom Newland loved but renounced. In order to stress this contrast between the customs of the two ages, she describes the world Fanny Beaufort lives in as more untrammeled by any customs than it is easy to believe possible or than Edith Wharton, of all people, could ever have seriously believed, and makes the later life of Fanny's father one of a responsible domesticity wholly inconsistent with the splendidly gross and unscrupulous man he has been throughout the novel.

But these limiting displays of cleverness are insignificant in the book and never affect the main action. Throughout that action her intelligence, with its cultivated powers of analysis and construction, is used to give dramatic emphasis to the experience of characters and ways of life that are alive in her imagination. The difference that

G

makes is evident in the success she has with the love affair of Newland
Archer and Ellen Olenska, whose passion and whose refusal to be
self-deceived she makes beautifully vivid and convincing. Having
made us see the insights and ignorances both of them have acquired
from the ways they have lived, she also makes us believe completely
in the undeveloped powers of both that make their love for one another almost inevitable, and the frustration of that love inescapable.
It would be hard to overpraise the dramatic skill and economy with
which she brings these things about. The novel's opening sequence of
scenes illustrates them clearly. In addition to establishing the senses of
life that govern Newland Archer and Ellen Olenska, these scenes
must create for us the context in which their love has its existence,
the little world in which old New York, with its incurious ignorance
of great reaches of reality, is conducting its stubborn, doomed battle
to resist the encroachments of the powerful, unscrupulous, and often
brutal *nouveaux riches,* whose ambition it is to be a part of old New
York society.

Mrs. Wharton begins with a scene in the old Academy of Music.
"Conservatives cherished [the old Academy] for being small and in-
convenient, and thus keeping out the 'new people' whom New York
was beginning to dread and yet be drawn to." Into the "club" box at
the old Academy comes Newland Archer, a young man with a capacity for reality who has awakened from the long sleep of his society
only enough to be a dilettante. While Madame Nilsson is, as convention requires, trilling the Italian translation of *Faust*—*"M'ama . . .
non m'ama"*—Newland glances over at the box of old Mrs. Manson
Mingott, the daring but not too daring old lady who rules the family
Newland is engaged to marry into, looking for her granddaughter and
his fiancée, May Welland, the charming, Dianalike, conventional girl
of his choice. There she is, her eyes lowered "to the immense bouquet
of lilies-of-the-valley" Newland has sent her; it is all most satisfactory
—until there suddenly slips into the box a slim young woman in what
strikes New York as a most unusual dress, "a dark blue velvet gown

rather theatrically caught up under her bosom by a girdle with an old-fashioned clasp."

With the quiet assurance of her unconventional beauty and her cosmopolitan training, Ellen Olenska is unaware of the provincial astonishment her appearance arouses in old New York. Back there for the first time since her childhood after a brilliant and desperately unhappy European marriage, she sees these people as children, innocently good and harmless ("I see everybody here in knickerbockers and pantalettes"), a refuge she longs for. She is at once simpler and more subtle than they, so that when she comes to the formidable dinner given by the leaders of New York society, the van der Luydens, she arrives late, "one hand still ungloved, and fastening a bracelet about her wrist; yet she entered without any appearance of haste or embarrassment." Later, quite unconscious of New York social customs in this matter, she calmly crosses the room to sit next to Newland and—when they are interrupted—says composedly, "Tomorrow, then, at five—I shall expect you," though no engagement has been mentioned.

To New York, with its savage's passion for a rigid etiquette and an elaborate indirection, her unostentatious directness is altogether baffling. Even to Newland Archer, even after he has come to know her well, it is a constant surprise. When, thinking of the dullness of New York, he says he wonders she does not go back to the exquisite life of Europe despite the horrors of life with her husband and she answers simply, "I believe it is because of you," he is astonished, even though "it was imposible to make the confession more dispassionately, or in a tone less encouraging to the vanity of the person addressed." For like all she says, when she says anything at all, this is the simple truth; it is Newland who has made her understand that "under the dullness [of New York life] there are things so fine and sensitive and delicate that even those I most cared for in my other life look cheap in comparison."

When this woman, with her odd beauty, her subtle simplicity, and her hopeful faith in the goodness of old New York society, walks into the Mingott box, we hear the voice of old Sillerton Jackson, New York's great social arbiter, saying, "I didn't think the Mingotts would have tried it on." That comment is a measure of Ellen's misunderstanding of them, but it is also a measure of their own moral confusion, for this remark immediately precedes the departure of everyone who counts from the crumbling protection of the old Academy of Music to the ball at the luxurious house of Julius Beaufort, who has, with his confident extravagance, won his way into old New York society. There is something almost admirable about the cynical defiance with which Julius Beaufort has hung his scandalous nude, Bouguereau's "Love Victorious," just where all his guests will have to take a good look at it as they arrive at the ball. We see clearly that old New York is much more likely to exclude the alien superiority of Ellen Olenska than the alien corruption of Julius Beaufort.

When we have reached the Beaufort house with Newland and have strolled through "the sea-green, the crimson, the *bouton d'or*" drawing rooms (in the last of which hangs "Love Victorious") and lingered momentarily in the "library hung with Spanish leather and furnished with Buhl and malachite," we arrive in a ballroom that is vivid with "the dashing aigrettes and ornaments of the young married women's coiffures." There we find May Welland with her bouquet of lilies-of-the-valley announcing with innocent boldness her engagement to Newland, in order that the Archers may come openly to the support of the Mingotts in countenancing her dubious, Europeanized cousin Ellen, who has not the faintest suspicion that she needs countenancing.

In this easy and richly conscious way, Mrs. Wharton sets up her novel's central situation. There is Newland Archer, caught between the innocent idealism and the carefully cultivated imperceptiveness of May Welland that appeals to all there is in him of the habitual New York idea of life, and the subtle simplicity of Ellen Olenska that appeals to all the possibilities within him for a full life. Each of these women is in turn placed between Newland and an almost equally powerful force pulling her in the opposite direction. For May Welland that force is her family with its promise of the delicious safety of a stupidly conventional life; for Ellen it is Julius Beaufort, who immediately makes a dead set for her, with his confident if brutalizing command of the great world and its "exquisite pleasures."

It is Mrs. Wharton's ability really to create these lives, rather than merely to assert that they exist, that makes *The Age of Innocence* so moving. When Newland and Ellen have their day together at Point Arley—their single escape from the stifling social world of New York and Newport—she makes us enter fully into the dazzling exhilaration that unexpectedly united lovers know, without platitude of statement or idle irony, by a simple but wholly right representation of what they do. As they ride the ferry to Point Arley, Newland is wise enough to keep silent, aware that they have achieved the only kind of nearness their circumstances permit and the essential—if not the only necessary—expression of their love. Then, with masculine lack of patience, he destroys that silence. "What's the use?" he says savagely, in almost the exact words Mrs. Wharton had written about Walter Berry a dozen years before. "You gave me my first glimpse of a real life, and at that same moment you asked me to go on with a sham one. It's beyond human enduring—that's all." At this Ellen, for the first time, gives herself away, not by an act of self-surrender but by a reassertion of the value of their renunciation. "Oh, don't say that," she bursts out, "when I'm enduring it." Then Edith Wharton finds a wonderful line to express the amazement and the pain of Newland's understanding of all she has felt. "You too—oh, all this time, you, too?"

Ellen is determined that they shall not deceive themselves. When she returns from Washington to care for old Mrs. Mingott and Newland drives her from the railroad station to Mrs. Mingott's house, he rebels again. "I want somehow," he says, "to get away with you into a world where . . . we shall be simply two human beings who love each other . . . and nothing else on earth will matter." "Oh, my dear," Ellen says, "—where is that country? Have you ever been there? I know so many who have tried to find it . . . and it wasn't at all different from the old world they'd left, but only rather smaller and

dingier and more promiscuous." It is one of the novel's innumerable
evidences of Mrs. Wharton's profound hold on her story that the first
time Newland had been deeply moved by Ellen he had been swept by
an uncritical feeling that he was with "someone who was bargaining
for attar-of-roses in Samarkand," and that the New York he was
actually in and the May Welland he was actually engaged to had con-
veniently become as remote and improbable as Samarkand in fact is.
The fine precision of the language in passages like these, its eloquent
communication of a sadness of renunciation made wholly convincing
by a vivid representation of what is renounced, is the final reward of
Mrs. Wharton's commitment to her imagination in *The Age of Innocence*.

But beautifully realized as the mature passion and the moral realism of Ellen and Newland are, they are less unusual achievements
than Mrs. Wharton's success with the relation that balances this one,
the solid reality of the affection, the consideration and generosity, of
the quite ordinary, imperfect marriage of May and Newland. If Newland could not help loving Ellen but could renounce her in order not
to betray May, May could not help being imperceptive and earnestly
conventional but could rise to heights of inarticulate courage, as she
did when she offered Newland his freedom. (It is marvelously right
that May's conventional mind cannot conceive an occasion for that
offer more significant than Newland's trivial and forgotten dalliance
with poor Mrs. Thorley Rushworth.) We are made to feel too the
unglamorous but quite real tenderness with which Newland surrenders
the thing he had most wanted in his life, Ellen Olenska, because May
has asked him to. Not that she ever asked or he ever agreed in so many
words; it is not until May has been long dead that Newland accidentally discovers she understood. Then "it seemed to take an iron
band from his heart to know that, after all, someone had guessed and
pitied. . . . And that it should have been his wife moved him inde-
scribably."

When a novelist can create characters with feelings at once as relevant to her purpose and as deeply moving as these, every bit of in-

telligence she brings to the organization of them is pure gain, and
what is often only impressive skill in Mrs. Wharton's other books—
the ingenious plotting, the precise ordering of the action, the minute
observation of details of setting—becomes in *The Age of Innocence*
a means of giving dramatic focus to conduct and motives not arbitrarily invented to serve the requirements of a clever plot but found
by the imagination in the characters themselves and only then organized into an action. It is thus that *The Age of Innocence* earns the
bleak view of human experience that dominates it and that was, perhaps, Mrs. Wharton's deepest response to her own experience. This
view becomes explicit only in the final chapter of the book, which is
a kind of epilogue.

With the passion and the renunciation of Newland and Ellen fresh
in our minds from the final chapter of the story proper, in which we
are shown the dinner party at which old New York bids Ellen farewell
on her departure for Europe, we are abruptly confronted in this
epilogue with an occasion nearly thirty years later. Newland's wife,
May, is now dead and his son has carried him off to Paris, where, for
the first time since he and Ellen parted, he finds himself within reach
of her. By this means Mrs. Wharton makes the simple and terrible
truth, that time will come and take man's love away, a sharp dramatic surprise to us.

As Newland contemplates the situation, he thinks that Ellen will
have been unimaginably transformed by living for thirty years in a
highly cultivated world utterly alien to the man he has become by living for those thirty years the humdrum life he has known with May,
and we know he is right. We know he is right, too, when he thinks
that "perhaps [Ellen], too, had kept her memory of him as something
apart; but if she had it must have been like a relic in a small dim
chapel, where there was not time to pray every day." He and Ellen
had sacrificed the realization of their love to the sense of decency and
generosity that made it possible for them to love one another at all
"only if we stayed far from one another." Now, thirty years after,
they must face the truth that love kept apart in memory only, like a

relic, is, like all relics even for the truest believers, dead beyond revival except as a memory. Newland accepts this knowledge, and we are convinced that Ellen will too when Newland, having walked as far as Ellen's flat, refuses to go up to see her, and sends his son, Dallas, up instead. He knows that "his boy 'took after him' "; Dallas is the closest thing to the Newland Archer of Ellen's memory that exists. For them both, the terrible truth is, as Newland thinks, that "it is more real to me here than if I went up."

This epilogue is Edith Wharton's last and most explicit expression of her beautifully balanced sense, implicit everywhere in the book, that the only endurable life is the one that preserves the values that have governed Newland and Ellen's lives—values that can only develop slowly and therefore will exist only in a stable and traditional society—and that these values can be preserved only at the cost of gradually starving the individual emotions that give them life and significance. Edith Wharton's perception of this complex truth is something she had earned by learning to accept the whole of her own nature, as she had not been able to when she wrote *The Reef*, as she had not even wanted to when she wrote most of her earlier books. That understanding is so fully embodied in *The Age of Innocence* that the book is an achievement of a quite different order from the work of Mrs. Wharton the intellectual, attractive in its way though that work is too.

The Big Money

1936

The first half of the twentieth century was an unusually exciting time for American fiction, and when such writers as Faulkner, Fitzgerald, Hemingway, Lewis, and Dos Passos—all of whom were born between 1895 and 1898—emerge simultaneously, it is not easy to pick out one or two of them who fairly represent what has happened to the novel in their time. The problem is further complicated by the fact that the period is marked by an increasing historical awareness. This development is sometimes traced to the influence of Marx's historical determinism in the thirties, but apart from being itself an historical explanation, this one does not appear to fit the facts very well. Although it is never easy to be sure people have not been influenced by a way of thinking that is so widespread, often in almost unrecognizable forms, as Marxism was in the thirties, the habit of thinking historically seems to be as common with writers apparently untouched by Marxism—Faulkner, for example—as it is with writers like Dos Passos who were evidently strongly influenced by it. There is also some evidence that this habit was established before Marxism was widely thought about in this country. Perhaps it is simply a development of the general emphasis on the historical aspect of reality in the late-nineteenth century.

In any event, this development had two important consequences for the American novel. In the first place it meant that any writer concerned primarily with outer reality tended to think of that reality in historical terms, particularly in social and political terms, and to write with an eye on the characteristics of a society rather than on those of the small, self-contained group that interests the traditional novelist of manners. In the second place it meant that most writers in the period, whichever aspect of reality they were primarily committed to, were acutely conscious of what they were doing. This essentially historical sense of themselves led them to analyze their own sense of reality and to express it in more sophisticated ways; it also made them aware of the other sense of reality and anxious to include some show of it in their novels. Thus Dos Passos conscientiously presents in the "Camera Eye" sections of *U.S.A.* a subjective, inner view of the experience he is describing, and Faulkner, despite his commitment to the subjective reality of his inner vision, makes "his story of Yoknapatawpha County stand as a parable of all the Deep South."

Dos Passos is a particularly interesting example of this complication of intentions and of the novelties of expression it entailed. Although his novels were concerned almost from the beginning with large historical occasions and although his feelings about them have always been essentially social ones, he began his career by trying to discover the meaning of such occasions in their aesthetic value for the private souls of extremely sensitive young men, and however far from this sense of reality the major emphasis in his novels later became, he has never wholly omitted it from his work. It is, indeed, possible to argue—as one or two critics such as T. K. Whipple and Malcolm Cowley did as early as the thirties, when Dos Passos was producing his most important work—that even the painstakingly objective narratives of his trilogies are as much fables for his sense of private reality as they are expressions of his sense of public reality, "furious and sombre poem[s], written in a mood of revulsion even more powerful than that which T. S. Eliot expressed in 'The Waste Land,' " as Malcolm Cowley put it when *The Big Money* appeared in 1936.

Dos Passos' novels are out of fashion at the moment, partly because his later work is inferior to the work he did in the thirties, but largely because the sense of private reality is momentarily the fashion in the intellectual marketplace, where an astonishing number of one-time intellectual Leftists are busy burning their old political draft cards for newspaper reporters and making a public career out of the happy conviction that their private experience—especially of political events —is not as that of other men. But this violent shift of attitude among the couturiers of the intellectual world ought not to conceal from us the importance for the American novel of Dos Passos' work or of the sense of reality it expresses.

Dos Passos began his career with three minor novels that are quite typical of their time. They are mainly accounts of the shocked horror with which sensitive and idealistic young men confront a society that is hopelessly vulgar and brutally unconcerned with their feelings about it. The most revealing of these early novels is *Three Soldiers* (1921), because it has, at least in a simplified form, the characteristic design Dos Passos was to give his later work. *Three Soldiers* describes the related careers of three American boys during the first world war. The first is an Italian-American named Fuselli, a conformist whose only desire is to succeed and be promoted. The second, Chrisfield, is a farm boy who cannot endure the mechanical regimentation of army life and is continually breaking out into violent, incoherent rebellion. The third and most important—he has obvious biographical over-tones—is John Andrews, an introverted young man filled with a yearning for Beauty of an almost 1890's kind.

When the Armistice is signed, Andrews finds himself in Paris with practically no duties, but the mere wearing of his uniform is so inhibiting to him that he deserts in order to be free to write a symphony. When the M.P.'s catch up with him he admits he is a deserter, and after a last devout look at "the windmill . . . turning, turning, against the piled white clouds of the sky" he goes quietly off to his doom. "On John Andrews's writing table the brisk wind rustled among the broad sheets of paper [his symphony]. First one sheet, then another, blew off the table, until the floor was littered with them."

Even these few details reveal the way Dos Passos broadened all his effects until they became normative, even those that ostensibly represent the unique private feelings of John Andrews. Like the windmill and the white clouds, John Andrews's symphony never exists for the reader as an activity of his creative imagination, as part of the life of his inner self. It is only as real as those broad sheets of paper that constitute its public existence, the neglect of which demonstrates in an obvious, symbolic way the brutal indifference of organized society to the refinement John Andrews stands for.

What is striking about *Three Soldiers*—apart from its commitment to a sentimental aesthetic attitude—is the painstaking, almost diagrammatic design Dos Passos imposes on the story, a design that forces us to see his three main characters as representative rather than individual, almost as the types of some morality play. Psychologically each of them is reduced to the general attitude toward life he represents; Dos Passos relentlessly makes their every thought and act a manifestation of that attitude. They are caricatures, though deadly serious ones, and such complication of meaning as the novel has is produced by the conflicts among the attitudes represented by the characters; no convincing conflict occurs within any of them, nor is the inner reality of their experience—despite John Andrews's extravagant commitment to the private value of his aesthetic responses —ever given any life. It is easy enough to see now that what weakens *Three Soldiers* is its lack of any ground solider than aesthetic sensitivity for its rebellion against the regimented life of the ordinary world that is dramatized by life in the army. In his next novel, *Manhattan Transfer,* Dos Passos found that ground in a concern for the social values of American society.

This concern came more easily to him than to most writers of his generation. His father was a successful lawyer and Dos Passos was educated at Harvard, but as his name shows, John Roderigo Dos Passos came of immigrant stock and had a natural sympathy for the largely alien population that still constituted the working classes of America in his time. He found it easy to concentrate his idealism on the ambitions for a better life of people like these and to dedicate his work to a vision of social justice compounded out of the immigrant's hopes of America and the native American ideal of a democratic society that haunted earlier American novelists like Cooper and Mark Twain.

Manhattan Transfer is focused on the conflict between the conventional life of American society and the common man's vague ambition to lead a decent life in a just society, an ambition that is slowly but irresistibly transformed by the society into a desire for a conventional success that, when it is achieved, leaves the common man unfulfilled and confused by his unhappiness. It is a picture of the great American way station, New York City, in the 1920's, but this picture is made up of the private lives of a series of representative people, and it is deliberately constructed in such a way as to make its point by emphasizing the parallels and contrasts of their lives, just as is *Three Soldiers.*

But in *Manhattan Transfer* Dos Passos uses not three, but eight major characters as well as a host of significant minor ones, and these characters are no longer merely general types—the urban conformist, the independent farmer, the alienated aesthete. They are precisely defined social types—the country boy who cannot find his way in the city, starves, and commits suicide; the "Wizard of Wall Street" who plays the market once too often and ends begging in the streets; a wealthy paving contractor and a radical labor organizer; a successful actress who is happy neither with the man she loves, the impresario for whom she leaves him, nor the journalist she finally marries. With characters like these who are sharply defined and familiar social types, it is easy to see how remarkable Dos Passos' special gifts are, how skillfully he selects actions and feelings for his characters that surprise us with their truth to an experience we had thought uniquely ours and that at the same time show how representative these characters are of the social attitudes of their time and place.

Dos Passos' method is to take up the life of each of these characters in turn, follow it closely for a few years from the character's own point of view, and then shift to another character. He uses every possible opportunity to connect the lives of these characters, and the novel's "unity of place" provides a good many. The result is a novel with many interwoven plots, each centered on a major character with a point of view so fully developed that we understand and sympathize with his life, whether we approve of it or not. Yet the purpose of this web of lives is not, finally, to make us understand the individual characters, and Dos Passos never allows us to become so deeply involved with their private conceptions of their lives that we lose track of their public significance. There is a pervasive irony in his way of writing about them that always reminds us—at the very moment we are touched by the earnestness and sincerity of a character's commitment to an attitude—how typical, how representative, the attitude is. Each of these lives is, we see, characteristic of its time and place; and, taken together, they constitute an image of urban existence in the 1920's, when urban existence was beginning to be the characteristic form of American life.

An exactly similar purpose and a very similar method govern Dos Passos' most important work, the two trilogies with which he followed *Manhattan Transfer*. The first of these is called *U.S.A.* and was written between 1930 and 1936; the second is called *District of Columbia* and was written between 1939 and 1949. These six novels cover the social and political life of America during the first half of the twentieth century. The best of them is the last one of the first trilogy, which covers the 1920's and is called *The Big Money*.

The central narrative of *The Big Money* has Dos Passos' familiar form, a design of interwoven, representative lives. Here again it is his remarkable eye for vivid yet typical details and his social irony that give the narrative its force, as when he shows us Charley Anderson, a Minnesota boy who has been a brilliant wartime flyer, at his first postwar New York party.

> They had white wine with the fish and red wine with the roast-beef and a dessert all full of whippedcream. Charley kept telling himself he mustn't drink too much so that he'd be sure to behave right. . . .
>
> After dinner [Miss Humphries] and Charley took their coffee-cups into a window bay behind a big pink begonia in a brass pot and she asked him if he didn't think New York was awful. She sat on the windowseat and he stood over her looking past her white shoulder through the window down at the traffic in the street below. It had come on to rain and the lights of the cars made long rippling streaks on the black pavement of Park Avenue. . . . He was wondering if it would be all right if he told her she had beautiful shoulders. He'd just about gotten around to it when he heard Ollie Taylor getting everybody together to go out to a cabaret.

But *The Big Money* also uses three devices Dos Passos invented for *U.S.A.* The first of these is called "the Newsreel." It is a mixture of newspaper headlines and advertising slogans, sentences from magazine articles and political speeches, and snatches of popular songs, all drawn from the moment of social history that Dos Passos is dealing with in his main narrative. The Newsreel is a verbal collage, a folk poem for industrial society. Here are the vague hopes of ordinary men exactly as they are misrepresented by the Tin Pan Alley songwriters and the Sunday-supplement writers of the day; here are the solemn pronouncements of the "responsible" opinion-makers who are bent on keeping ordinary men in their places and are listened to earnestly by such men, and the angry eloquence of "irresponsible" revolutionaries who want to help ordinary men and are scornfully ignored by them.

What Dos Passos can do with this ironic kind of public poem is shown by the first Newsreel in *The Big Money*. It deals with 1919, when Charley Anderson was arriving in New York and the opinion-makers were greatly disturbed by the radicalism of the returning sol-diers, and the radical press was attacking the dominance of the fed-

eral government by large corporations like the United States Steel
Corporation; when Charles M. Schwab of the Steel Company was advising President Wilson about how to keep businessmen happy and
Wilson's heroic effort to persuade the country to accept the League
of Nations ended in a stroke—and George M. Cohan was making a
tremendous hit in New York with a patriotic musical comedy called
Yankee Doodle Dandy.

Yankee Doodle that melodee

TO CONQUER SPACE AND SEE DISTANCES

but has not the time come for newspaper proprietors to join in a
wholesome movement for the purpose of calming troubled minds,
giving all the news but laying less stress on prospective calamities

DEADLOCK UNBROKEN AS FIGHT SPREADS

they permitted the Steel Trust Government to trample underfoot
the democratic rights which they had so often been assured were
the heritage of the people of this country

SHIPOWNERS DEMAND PROTECTION

Yankee doodle that melodee
Yankee doodle that melodee
Makes me stand right up and cheer. . . .

PRESIDENT STRONGER WORKS IN SICK ROOM

I'm coming U. S. A.
I'll say

MAY GAG PRESS

There's no land . . . so grand

Charles M. Schwab, who has returned from Europe, was a
luncheon guest at the White House. He stated that this country

was prosperous but not so prosperous as it should be, because there were so many disturbing investigations on foot

> *. . . as my land*
> *From California to Manhattan Isle*

Just as the Newsreel makes poems out of the public experience of moments of social history, so Dos Passos' second technical invention, called "the Camera Eye," makes poetry out of Dos Passos' own private feelings about such moments. Late in *The Big Money* one of the characters is involved in the unsuccessful effort made by American liberals in 1927 to save the lives of Sacco and Vanzetti, two working-class Italian anarchists who were accused of having killed a man during a hold-up and sentenced to the electric chair by the Commonwealth of Massachusetts.

Dos Passos had been deeply involved in the Sacco-Vanzetti affair, and one of the Camera Eye passages represents the flow of his thoughts and feelings as he walked one day from Plymouth, Massachusetts, where the first Pilgrims had landed in the seventeenth century, to North Plymouth, where, in the twentieth century, Bartolomeo Vanzetti had worked for the Plymouth Cordage Company until he was fired for being a Red and became a fish-peddler.

> this is where the immigrants landed the roundheads the sackers of castles the kingkillers haters of oppression . . . on the beach that belonged to no one   between the ocean that belonged to no one and the enormous forest that belonged to no one that stretched over the hills . . . forever into the incredible west
>   for threehundred years the immigrants toiled into the west and now today
>   walking from Plymouth to North Plymouth suddenly round a bend in the road . . . you see the Cordage . . . sharply ranked squares and oblongs cutting off the sea   the Plymouth Cordage
>   this is where another immigrant worked hater of oppression who wanted a world unfenced   when they fired him from the Cordage he peddled fish. . . . Don't let them scare you   make them feel who are your oppressers America

rebuild the ruined words worn slimy in the mouths of lawyers
districtattorney collegepresidents judges   without the old
words the immigrants haters of oppression brought to Plymouth
how can you know who are your betrayers America
or that this fishpeddler you have in Charlestown Jail is one of
your founders Massachusetts?

The third new device Dos Passos uses in *U.S.A.* is the brief, emotionally charged "Biography" of a representative public figure of the
time. In *The Big Money* there are biographies of Frederick Winslow
Taylor, who invented time-and-motion studies and became the first
efficiency expert; Henry Ford, who invented mass production; Thor-
stein Veblen, the brilliant and eccentric sociologist who wrote *The
Theory of the Leisure Class;* Isadora Duncan, the dancer who was
half genius and half crank; Rudolph Valentino, the movie idol; the
Wright Brothers, who first flew an airplane; Frank Lloyd Wright, the
age's crotchety architectural genius; William Randolph Hearst, the
fabulously wealthy inventor of America's yellow press; and Samuel
Insull, who built a huge and crooked utilities empire. Nearly every
significant aspect of American society in the 1920's is represented in
this list. The Biography of Veblen is typical of the way Dos Passos
treats these people.

Veblen
asked too many questions, suffered from a constitutional inability to say yes.
Socrates asked questions, drank down the bitter drink one night
when the first cock crowed,
but Veblen
drank it in little sips through a long life in the stuffiness of class-
rooms, the dust of libraries, the staleness of cheap flats such as a
poor instructor could afford. He fought the bogy all right, ped-
antry, routine, timeservers at office desks, trustees, collegepresidents, the plump flunkies of the ruling businessmen, all the good
jobs kept for yesmen, never enough money, every broadening hope
thwarted. Veblen drank the bitter drink all right.

All three of these technical innovations are devices for emphasizing in a dramatic way the general social significance of individual men's experiences. The Newsreel gives us the ironic poetry of journalism's crude public image of that experience; the Biography gives us the individual experience of a socially significant public figure; and the Camera Eye gives us the author's own immediate experience of socially important events. Dos Passos uses these devices to punctuate the main narrative.

The main narrative consists of the lives of three typical Americans of the twenties. The first of the three we meet is Charley Anderson, a big, handsome country boy from Minnesota who is thrust suddenly into the world of the Big Money when he arrives back in New York after the war surrounded by the temporary glamor of his heroic achievements as a flier. For a short time he enjoys the role of returning hero and finds himself enthralled by the luxury of New York. He finds the delicate and—as he never does see—coldly selfish women of this world enormously appealing. Dos Passos is insistent that the straightforward, vigorous sexuality of the simple Minnesota boy has been badly warped by the luxury that is a part of the special appeal of these women. It is a curious and interesting point, one that keeps reappearing in American fiction of the twentieth century—for example, in Dreiser's *An American Tragedy* and Fitzgerald's *The Great Gatsby,* in both of which wealth and sex get muddled in the heroes' imaginations and give certain women a false glamor for them.

After this brief interlude in New York, Charley Anderson goes back to St. Paul and takes the job as a mechanic in the Ford garage where he had worked before the war. In a half-hearted way he also takes up with the girl he had been involved with then. But this life seems to him unbearably dull after his taste of the world of the Big Money and he takes the first opportunity that comes along to get back to New York, a chance to be a partner in a company—financed by one of Charley's wartime friends—that is going to make an airplane self-starter invented by Charley.

For a year or so Charley works like a dog at the plant—he is a really gifted mechanic—and the company flourishes. But then he begins to pursue an upper-class New York girl and it becomes plain to him that he is going to need big money quickly if he is not to lose her. He neglects his job at the plant in order to gamble on the stock market, but though he is lucky, the girl throws him over anyway. He then goes on a bender and while he is still drunk, gives the control of the company to a big Detroit firm by selling his stock to them, without consulting his partner, and takes a $25,000-a-year job with the people he has sold out to. In Detroit he marries a girl very like the one that had thrown him over in New York and is badly hurt when his old partner in New York, whom he has asked to be his best man, wires him a succinct "No."

He quickly comes to hate the pseudo-elegant parties his wife gives and is happy only when he is drinking too much with his old friends among the mechanics at the plant. Then he has a bad flying accident, and when he becomes a serious handicap to his wife's social life, she ships him off to Florida to recuperate. By this time he is a florid, overweight, overdressed businessman who drinks too much, though he still thinks of himself—when he has drunk enough—as a handsome young man who can fly a plane and drive a car with dazzling skill; in these moments he is naïvely confident that he can defeat those who in some obscure way have cheated him—his wife, his business associates, life. In his innocently unconsidering way, Charley has accepted the popular values of his decade, the belief in the supreme desirability of the world of the Big Money, though he finds no pleasure in its activities. In order to buy his way into that world he lives the nerve-racking life of management politics and brokers' offices rather than the creative mechanic's life that he understands.

In Florida he picks up a pretty actress named Margo Dowling, who is the novel's third main character, speculates in the Florida land boom of the middle twenties under the guidance of a Southern senator who is a good deal cleverer and more unscrupulous than Charley, and becomes a lush. His wife uses his relations with Margo Dowling to get a profitable divorce and to separate him from his children, and he is frozen out of the Detroit company when he goes off on a bender and is not able to look after his interests during a market crisis. His end comes when he gets drunk in a Florida nightclub and picks up a stray girl whom he insists on showing what a marvelous driver he is. He finds himself driving alongside an express train and sets out to beat it to the next grade crossing. As he always has, Charley wins the race, and as always, gets run over, his car swerving out of control and stalling on the tracks just as the express arrives at the crossing. He dies without ever understanding what has happened to him.

As Kenneth Fearing, one of the poets of the thirties, put it about the type Charley Anderson represents,

> zowie did he live and zowie did he die,
> With who the hell are you at the corner of his casket, and
>   where the hell we going on the right-hand silver
>   knob, and who the hell cares walking second from
>   the end with an American Beauty wreath from why
>   the hell not, . . .
> Wham, Mr. Roosevelt; pow, Sears Roebuck; awk, big dipper;
>   bop, summer rain;
>   bong, Mr., bong, Mr. bong, Mr., bong.

Dos Passos' second major character is Mary French, who grows up in the middle west, the child of a selfless doctor and a socially ambitious mother. Mary goes to Vassar and becomes interested in social work when she hears a lecture there by a middle-aged professional liberal. She leaves college and goes to Chicago to work at Hull House, the famous social center founded by Jane Addams; from there she moves on to Pittsburgh, where she becomes deeply involved in helping the Polish steel workers as they go down to bitter defeat in one of the great strikes of the twenties. During the strike she runs into the professional liberal who had so deeply impressed her at Vassar; he is in Pittsburgh to help settle the strike, which he eventually does, by selling out the strikers. The strike is a bitterly disillusioning experience for Mary; the systematic and cynical lying of the employers and the brutality of the police, the poverty and the courage of the strikers, the futility of the self-deceiving liberals are a new discovery for her, convincing her that the class war is not going to be resolved by reason and good will but is a war without quarter that will have to be fought to the death.

In her shock and uncertainty she accepts a job as the secretary of the professional liberal and goes off to Washington with him, where she drifts into being his mistress. When she discovers she is pregnant she runs off to New York, has an abortion, and discovers the Communist Party, which seems to her the only group that is honestly facing the reality of the class war. She is quickly involved with a fiery young Communist spokesman named Ben Compton, who is at the moment fresh out of jail and a much publicized Party hero. But their affair is a short one: Ben is away too much speaking for the Party and Mary is too busy working at headquarters in New York. Then she meets a young Party leader named Don Stevens and falls deeply in love with him. Don rises rapidly in the Party and is presently sent secretly to Moscow. While she is waiting for him to come back, Mary runs into Ben Compton on the street, lost and woebegone because, in the fierce struggle for personal power within the Party that has shot Don Stevens to the top, Ben has been thrown out of it for some obscure heresy. Don comes back from Moscow with a new girl he has met there.

By this time it is 1927 and Mary goes off to Boston to work for Sacco and Vanzetti, and we live through with her the long agony of the losing struggle to save these two men who are to Mary the innocent victims of the governing classes' pitiless hatred of working-class idealists. Mary has her moment of exultation as she goes off to jail with the other demonstrators the night Sacco and Vanzetti are electrocuted, defiantly singing the "International" and remembering Vanzetti's final words—"If it had not been for these things I might have lived out my life talking at street corners to scorning men. I might have died unknown, unmarked, a failure. This is our career and our triumph. Never in our full life can we hope to do such work for tolerance, for justice, for man's understanding of man as now we do by an accident."

It is one of Dos Passos' most effective touches that the last we see of Mary French is not this moment of exultation. The last glimpse we have of her is at a fashionable New York cocktail party to which her old Vassar roommate has taken her "for a change." There she runs into the professional liberal who had been her first lover and the now fading movie star, Margo Dowling, who had been Charley Anderson's mistress and whose life constitutes Dos Passos' third major story.

Margo has been brought up in a small town near New York by a good-natured, hard-drinking father and a stepmother named Agnes. Fred simply disappears while Margo is a child and Agnes goes to live with a vaudeville actor who calls himself Frank Mandeville. Frank puts Margo, now a pretty young girl, into his act and, as soon as she is old enough, rapes her. To escape from this situation, Margo marries a handsome young Cuban named Tony who lives in the neighborhood and he takes her to Havana, where he becomes so interested in making a career for himself by catering to rich homosexuals that Margo has to fight her way free and come back to New York. There she returns to the stage and nearly marries a rich young Yale athlete, but at the last minute he deserts her in Florida, and there, when she is down to her last fifteen cents, Charley Anderson picks her up on his way to Miami and she lives with him until he is killed. Charley, though he tries hard enough, does not manage to leave her anything: even the five-thousand-dollar check he signs on his deathbed turns out to be no good.

Margo has had to become tough and shrewd in order to survive the life she is forced to live, but she remains a loyal and responsible person. She has recognized the pathos of Charley Anderson and has been fond of him despite his difficulty and foolishness; she knows that beneath Agnes's silliness, her stepmother is devoted and hard-working and she feels responsible for her; she even pities Tony, who, whenever he is in trouble, comes running to her for help. After Charley's death she sets bravely off for Hollywood, taking Agnes and Tony with her, in the hope of making a career there. For three weary years she gets nowhere; then she accidentally meets a man she had known when he was a young fashion photographer in New York and who is now a big director. He marries her and makes her a star. We do not see her again until she appears in the background at the New York cocktail party we go to with Mary French, where we hear someone telling Mary that Margo Dowling is through; sound has come in and Margo's voice is hopeless.

Like Charley Anderson, Margo Dowling is a fundamentally decent human being. She has lived from day to day doing what she had to to survive and she has ended as something she does not like being and would never have chosen to become. She is shrewder and more aware of what is happening to her than is Charley Anderson with his naïve delight in the Big Money or Mary French with her idealistic faith in its enemies; but she is as helpless as they are to keep it from shaping her life.

She is shrewd and brave and tough enough to succeed in the savage world that has defeated and destroyed Charley and Mary, but she is nonetheless its victim, essentially a commodity that can—and does—become obsolete overnight when there is a technological change. The choices that confronted Dos Passos' three characters have all been bad. They were free to sell what they had—their talents and their personal charms—for shoddy uses and to sacrifice their humanity for the sterile life of success in the world of the Big Money, as Charley and Margo did; or they could fight that world at the sacrifice of their own private lives, in a nightmare of overwork, by serving a cause that is constantly being corrupted from within by the hypocrisy of liberals and the cynical power-hunger of Communists; or they could become the anonymous vagrant, thumbing his way westward along the highway in depression America, with whom Dos Passos ends *The Big Money*.

Despite Dos Passos' commitment to the kind of outer reality represented by social history, despite his sympathy with the radical political tradition that has persisted throughout American history, he writes neither social history nor political propaganda. Behind his image of American society in the 1920's is an image of human experience as a whole; behind his political dislike of the Big Money is a despair of the human situation itself that justifies Malcolm Cowley's description of *The Big Money* as "a furious and sombre poem." If his wonderfully particularized, brilliantly organized portrait of America in the boom years of the twenties shows us what the Big Money does to simple, hopeful Americans, it also suggests what organized society does to all such men in·all times.

Dos Passos is the only major American novelist of the twentieth century who has had the desire and the power to surround the lives of his characters with what Lionel Trilling once called "the buzz of history"—the actual, homely, everyday sounds of current events and politics, of social ambitions and the struggle for money, of small pleasures and trivial corruptions, amidst which we all live. He has given us an image of a major aspect of our experience that has hardly been touched by any other novelist of our time.

F. SCOTT FITZGERALD
1896-1940

Tender Is the Night

1934

F. Scott Fitzgerald was the first of the gifted American novelists of the 1920's to become famous; he had a Byronic, overnight success with his first novel, *This Side of Paradise,* which was published in the first year of the decade. It was a brash, immature novel that Fitzgerald's lifelong friend Edmund Wilson called "one of the most illiterate books of any merit ever published." Later in his life Fitzgerald himself said of it, with the queer impersonality he could always give his considered judgments of himself, "A lot of people thought it was a fake, and perhaps it was, and a lot of others thought it was a lie, which it was not."

The essential quality of Fitzgerald's insight is shown by that comment. Looked at objectively, *This Side of Paradise* was in many ways a fake; it pretended to all sorts of knowledge and experience of the world its author did not in fact have. But it was not a lie; it expressed with accuracy and honesty its author's inner vision of himself and his experience, however false to literal fact that vision might be at certain points. Fitzgerald's reality was always that inner vision, but he had a deep respect for the outer reality of the world because it was the only place where his inward vision could be fulfilled, could be made actual.

The tension between his inescapable commitment to the inner reality of his imagination and his necessary respect for the outer reality of the world is what gives his fiction its peculiar charm and is the source of his ability to surround a convincing representation of the actual world with an air of enchantment that makes the most ordinary occasions haunting.

The success of *This Side of Paradise* did not do Fitzgerald any good. It gave him the fame and money to plunge into the gay whirl of New York parties that in postwar America somehow seemed to be a more significant life than the provincial one prewar America had lived. Fitzgerald and his beautiful wife, Zelda, rode through New York on the tops of taxis, jumped fully clothed into the Pulitzer Fountain in front of the Plaza, and quickly became leaders among the bright spirits of postwar New York. It was all harmless enough in itself, but it left very little time for serious writing, particularly for a man to whom alcohol was very damaging, almost a poison.

Yet all the time Fitzgerald was busy being the handsome hero of the Younger Generation, there was a serious writer inside him struggling to get out. That serious writer got control for a moment when he wrote *The Great Gatsby* (1924). But then the Fitzgeralds fell back into the life of parties—now mostly in Paris and on the Riviera—that gradually became for them a more and more desperate and self-destructive effort to be happy. It ended in 1930, when Zelda became a serious schizophrene and Fitzgerald, pulled up short by this disaster, found himself an alcoholic. He spent the rest of his brief life—he died in 1940, shortly after his forty-fourth birthday—fighting a grim battle to save Zelda, to cure his own alcoholism, and to fulfill his promise as a writer. "I have been a poor caretaker of everything I possessed," he said at this time, "even of my talent." He lost Zelda—she never grew better—and he was only partly successful in his fight against alcoholism. But, sick and discouraged though he was, he managed before he died to write *Tender Is the Night,* published in 1934, and a marvelous fragment of another novel called *The Last Tycoon.*

Tender Is the Night has certain defects traceable to the conditions

in which it was written. As Fitzgerald himself said of it with his remarkable honesty, "If a mind is slowed up ever so little, it lives in the
individual parts of a book rather than in a book as a whole; memory
is dulled. I would give anything if I hadn't had to write Part III of
'Tender Is the Night' entirely on stimulant." Despite these defects,
Tender Is the Night is the most mature and moving book Fitzgerald
ever wrote.

It is not, however, an easy book to understand. Its difficulty is at
least partly due to the odd discrepancy in it between the almost friv-
olous insignificance—by conventional standards anyhow—of the
hero's life and the importance Fitzgerald obviously means us to at-
tach to it. This difficulty in *Tender Is the Night* is only a particular
instance of the general problem created in American fiction by the
subjective novel as distinguished from the objective novel of social
history such as Dos Passos wrote.

Fitzgerald and Dos Passos were friends, but it is evident that neither
could understand what the other was up to. In 1933, the year before
Fitzgerald completed *Tender Is the Night,* he wrote a mutual friend,
"Dos was here, & we had a nice evening—we never quite understand
each other & perhaps that's the best basis for an enduring friendship."
As if to prove how right Fitzgerald was, Dos Passos wrote him, when
he published the revealing essays called "The Crack-Up" that describe
the personal experience underlying *Tender Is the Night,* "I've been
wanting to see you, naturally, to argue about your *Esquire* articles—
Christ, man, how do you find time in the middle of the general con-
flagration to worry about all that stuff? . . . most of the time the
course of world events seems so frightful that I feel absolutely para-
lysed." Clearly, Dos Passos is baffled by Fitzgerald's preoccupation
"with all that stuff" about the meaning of his personal experience.
Fitzgerald was equally baffled by Dos Passos' obsession with "the
course of world events."

There was of course a subjective novelist somewhere in Dos Passos, but Dos Passos relegated this novelist to the Camera Eye passages
of *U.S.A.* and he affects the narrative only indirectly. There was also

a man with a considerable sense of history in Fitzgerald: as Malcolm Cowley once put it, Fitzgerald lived in a room full of clocks and calendars. But Fitzgerald's knowledge of history, astonishing as his memory for it was, gets into his novels almost entirely as metaphors for the life of his consciousness, for the quality of his private experience. His summary of the year 1927—the year in which the slow decline of Dick Diver, the hero of *Tender Is the Night,* becomes clearly evident—is characteristic:

> By 1927 a wide-spread neurosis began to be evident, faintly signalled, like a nervous beating of the feet, by the popularity of cross-word puzzles. I remember a fellow expatriate opening a letter from a mutual friend of ours, urging him to come home and be revitalized by the hardy, bracing qualities of the native soil. It was a strong letter and it affected us both deeply, until we noticed that it was headed from a nerve sanitarium in Pennsylvania.

Fitzgerald tended to notice only those events that had this kind of meaning for him, that came to life for him as images of his personal feelings. The advantage of knowing the world in this way is that anything you notice at all takes on the vividness of your strongest private emotions. But because Fitzgerald knew the world this way, he had little capacity for sharing the common, public understanding of it. For readers to whom a novel is a dramatic representation of the world as that understanding knows it, Fitzgerald often appears to be treating with ridiculous seriousness characters and situations that "everyone knows" are insignificant.

One can frequently see in Fitzgerald's actual life, where conventional judgments are more important—or at least more difficult to ignore—how little such judgments really counted for him. All his life, for instance, he remembered bitterly his failure to achieve social success as an undergraduate at Princeton. The conventional judgment is that undergraduate social life is trivial, but Fitzgerald's failure at Princeton—whatever common sense may say of its circumstances—involved his deepest private feelings. Princeton was his first independent experience of the world, and he threw himself into realizing his ambitions there exactly as if Princeton had been the great world itself. For him the common judgment of Princeton's unimportance did not count; what counted was what he felt. He came very close to succeeding at Princeton, except that he neglected what was to him the trifling business of passing his courses, which seemed to him a great bore, and just as he was about to come into his kingdom as a big man on campus, he was forced to leave the university.

He tried for the rest of his life to tell himself that society always has this power to enforce its own values and that it was foolish of him to ignore the university's academic requirements simply because they were insignificant to him. But he never could really believe it, and gradually this experience at Princeton became for him—despite the objective insignificance of its occasion—one of his two or three major images for the unjust suffering that is the essence of human defeat.

This typical episode makes it evident that Fitzgerald, subjective novelist though he was, was not the kind of man who could commit himself wholly to the life of inner reality or be content as a novelist "with a very slight embroidery of outward manners, the faintest possible counterfeit of real life." In his life Fitzgerald strove to achieve in the actual world the ideal life he could so vividly imagine, and he was intent as a writer on producing the most lively possible counterfeit of real life.

But if this episode shows us that both in his life and his work he was determined to live in the actual world, as he often did quite dazzlingly, it also shows us that for him the meaning and value of the world were something that was determined by his private feelings, which operated independently of the established, conventional understanding of the world, not because he was consciously defying that understanding—his desire to realize the good life as he conceived it made him struggle to conform—but because the subjective life of his imagination was so intense, so overwhelmingly real for him, that even his efforts to conform to conventional ideas transformed them into something personal and queer.

Fitzgerald's first mature novel, *The Great Gatsby,* for example, is a brilliant picture of Long Island society in the 1920's. But that is only one aspect of it, the image Fitzgerald creates for a feeling too complex to be expressed in any other way. *The Great Gatsby* is a fable, marked at every important point by the folklore qualities of fables and charged with meaning by a style that is, despite the sharpness of its realistic detail, alive with poetic force. At the crisis of the story, the heroine, Daisy Buchanan, unintentionally reveals to her husband by the unguarded tone of her beautifully expressive voice that she loves Gatsby. The narrator says anxiously to Gatsby, "She's got an indiscreet voice. It's full of—" and when he hesitates Gatsby says suddenly, "Her voice is full of money." And the narrator thinks, "That was it. I'd never understood before. It was full of money— that was the inexhaustible charm that rose and fell on it, the jingle of it, the cymbals' song of it. . . . High in a white palace the king's daughter, the golden girl. . . ."

This passage is resonant with an irony that echoes back and forth between the gross actual fact of money jingling in the pocket and the romance of beauty adorned, of the golden girl. On the surface Daisy Buchanan is a convincing, historically accurate portrait of the charming and irresponsible upper-class girl of the American twenties. But she is also the princess, high in a white palace, for whom the disregarded younger son longs hopelessly, until the great moment when he astonishes everyone by performing the imposible feat that wins her hand.

One of the things that has certainly helped make *Tender Is the Night* less popular than *The Great Gatsby* of ten years earlier is that the image it uses, its story, is not, as social history, so significant as Gatsby's. Its story describes the life of well-to-do American expatriates on the Riviera during the 1920's, and such people are usually thought to be about as insignificant as Princeton undergraduates. They were especially thought to be so when the novel was published in 1934 at the depth of the Great Depression, and the idea that Fitzgerald was naïvely impressed by rich people became widely accepted. This is one of those foolish ideas put about by people who cannot read. Fitzgerald was no more a mere worshiper of rich people than Henry James was a snob. He was a man who dreamed of actually living the good life men can imagine. He had, as did Jay Gatsby, "a heightened sensitivity to the promises of life," and he had the elementary common sense to see that in real life the rich have an opportunity to live the good life that the rest of us do not.

One consequence of his seeing they do was that he felt the deepest scorn—what he called "the smouldering hatred of the peasant"—for rich people who did not take full advantage of the opportunity their wealth gave them. About rich people of this kind *Tender Is the Night* is devastating. Another consequence of it was his fascination with the intelligent and sensitive among the rich, like Dick Diver, who could see that opportunity. With his Irish sense of the absurd aspect of what he believed most deeply, Fitzgerald could make fun of this ideal as he had formulated it for himself, what he called "the Goethe-Byron-Shaw idea, with an opulent American touch—a sort of combination of Topham Beauclerk, St. Francis of Assisi, and J. P. Morgan"; and in the end he came to feel that the unimaginative brutality and organized chaos of the life of the rich always defeated men like Dick Diver. In Dick's best moments, *Tender Is the Night* shows us how beautiful the realized ideal life is; but in the end it shows us that people with the sensitivity and imagination to conceive that life cannot survive among the rich.

Tender Is the Night begins with the arrival of a young movie star named Rosemary Hoyt at Cap d'Antibes on the Riviera.* When Rosemary goes down to the beach she finds herself between two groups of expatriates. The first is an incoherent mixture. There is "Mama" Abrams, "one of those elderly 'good sports' preserved by an imperviousness to experience and a good digestion into another gen-

* There are two versions of *Tender Is the Night* in print, the original one described here and a revision based partly on a letter Fitzgerald wrote his editor late in his life and partly on a copy of the book found among his papers after he died, in which, along with some minor revisions in Book I, he had placed the original Book I after Book II Chapter 2.

eration." There is a writer named Albert McKisco who, according to his wife, Violet, is at work on a novel "on the idea of Ulysses. Only instead of taking twenty-four hours [he] takes a hundred years. He takes a decayed old French aristocrat and puts him in contrast with the mechanical age. . . ." There is a waspishly witty young man named Royal Dumphry and his companion, Luis Campion, who keeps admonishing Mr. Dumphry not to "be too ghastly for words." The other group consists of Dick Diver and his wife, Nicole, their friends Abe and Mary North, and a young Frenchman named Tommy Barban.

Rosemary is instinctively attracted to the second group but she is quickly picked up by the first group, who cannot wait to tell her they recognize her from her film. It is not a very happy group. For one thing, it is clearly jealous of the second group. "If you want to enjoy yourself here," Mrs. McKisco says, "the thing is to get to know some real French families. What do these people get out of it? They just stick around with each other in little cliques. Of course we had letters of introduction and met all the best French artists and writers in Paris." For another thing, Mr. McKisco is being difficult, as if, in spite of his extensive collection of secondhand attitudes from the best reviews, he does not quite know who he is or where he is going. When his wife makes a harmless joke, he bursts out irritably, "For God's sake, Violet, drop the subject! Get a new joke, for God's sake!" and when she leans over to Mrs. Abrams and says apologetically, "He's nervous," McKisco barks, "I'm not nervous. It just happens I'm not nervous at all."

It is the poverty of ideas and the mediocrity of imagination in these people, the shapelessness of their natures, that depresses and discomforts Rosemary and makes her dislike them. It is her glimpses of the opposite qualities in the second group that attracts her. What Rosemary sees in Dick Diver is his consideration, his grace, his sensitivity to others, and—behind them all—his intense vitality. No wonder she falls in love with him.

At this point Fitzgerald goes back to trace Dick's history. He is the son of a gentle, impoverished clergyman in Buffalo, from whom he had inherited his old-fashioned, formal manners and what Fitzgerald calls " 'good instincts,' honor, courtesy, courage." He has gone to Yale, been a Rhodes Scholar, and been trained as a psychiatrist at Johns Hopkins, in Vienna, and in Zurich. After the war, he returns to Zurich, where he meets again a young mental patient named Nicole Warren, who has clung to their slight relation all through the war and her slow recovery from an illness that is not congenital but has been brought on by her father's seducing her.

Dick falls in love with Nicole, and in spite of his professional knowledge that she may be a lifelong mental problem, despite the unconscious arrogance with which the Warrens make it clear they are buying a doctor to take care of Nicole, he marries her. This act reveals the defect of uncontrollable generosity in Dick's character. "He wanted," Fitzgerald says, "to be good, he wanted to be kind, he wanted to be brave and wise . . . ; [and] he wanted to be loved, too. . . ." He had an "extraordinary virtuosity with people . . . the power of arousing a fascinated and uncritical love." This power was a kind of imaginative unselfishness; "it was themselves he gave back to [people]," as Fitzgerald says, "blurred by the compromise of how many years." This power he could not resist exercising, not merely to give Nicole back her self but to make everyone he came close to feel once more the self he had been at his best.

Dick knows from the start that in taking up his life with Nicole among the Warrens and their kind he is making the task he has set himself as difficult as possible, but with his youthful vitality intact, that seems to him only to make it more challenging and interesting. For five years he meets that challenge effortlessly. Then, at first imperceptibly, his life begins to slip from his control. Something within him, some essential vitality, is beginning to decline, and he slowly realizes that he has exhausted the source of energy for the superb self-discipline that makes it possible for him to perform for others what he calls his "trick of the heart."

This change occurs very deep in his nature. Fitzgerald is careful to prevent the reader from thinking it is some change controllable by the will, some drift into dissipation or the idleness of the rich. Dick does begin to drift in these ways, but that is only a symptom of his trouble, a desperate search for something to fill the time and stave off boredom after the meaning and purpose have gone out of his life. What destroys Dick is something far more obscure and difficult to grasp, some spiritual malaise that is anterior to any rational cause and is—as has become much plainer since Fitzgerald noticed it—as widespread among sensitive people in our time as was accidie in the middle ages or melancholia, the "Elizabethan malady," in Shakespeare's. Dick Diver is, as Fitzgerald put it in one of his notes for the book, not simply an *homme manqué*, but an *homme epuisé*. He is in a state of terrible spiritual ennui that is without visible cause and yet makes men like him—talented, attractive, successful—feel quite literally that *all* the uses of the world are weary, stale, flat, and unprofitable. "I did not manage, I think in retrospect," Fitzgerald once said of Dick Diver, "to give Dick the cohesion I aimed at. . . . I wonder what the hell the first actor who played Hamlet thought of the part? I can hear him say, 'The guy's a nut, isn't he?' (We can always find great consolation in Shakespeare)."

Perhaps he did not manage to give Dick all the cohesion he might have, but the real difficulty is that the source of Dick's disaster is indescribable. It can be shown and felt, but it can no more be analyzed than Hamlet's disaster can. As a result the main action of *Tender Is the Night* is, for all its haunting emotional appeal, as puzzling and unparaphrasable as is the famous passage from Keats's *Ode to a Nightingale* from which its title comes.

What Fitzgerald can—and does—do is to create for the reader a group of characters who, as dramatic parallels or contrasts with Dick, show what he is. The first of these we learn all about is Abe North, a musician who, after a brilliant start, has done nothing for the last seven years except drink. When Mary North says, "I used to think until you're eighteen nothing matters," he says, "That's right. And afterwards it's the same way." And when Nicole, frightened at what he is doing to himself and irritated by his lack of any visible reasons for doing it, says to him, "I can't see why you've given up on everything," he can only say, "I suppose I got bored; and then it was such a long way to go back in order to get anywhere." Dick has understood from the beginning what has happened to Abe, even though he will not know what it feels like until later. "Smart men," he has said of Abe, "play close to the line because they have to—some of them can't stand it, so they quit." Thus, at the very start of the novel, Abe North has reached the point Dick will reach at its end.

About halfway through the novel, just as Dick is beginning his own desperate battle with the impulse to quit, he hears—in fact, he overhears, as a piece of idle, feelingless gossip—that Abe has been beaten up in a NewYork speakeasy and crawled to the Racket Club to die— or was it the Harvard Club? The gossips' grumbling quarrel over where it was Abe died fades out around Dick as he tries to face the meaning of Abe's death, a death more shocking—more grubby and humiliating as well as more terrifying to him—than anything he had dreamed of.

There is also Tommy Barban, a sophisticated and worldly barbarian of great charm, who stands for everything Dick Diver most disapproves of. The carefully ordered life that Dick first constructed for Nicole and himself because it was necessary to Nicole's health has, as Nicole's need for it has slowly decreased, been gradually transformed to another purpose, until it has become an alert but elaborate, almost ritualized ordering of the pleasures of a highly cultivated existence. The whole business irritates Tommy, partly because it is all strictly under Dick's control and holds Nicole, with whom Tommy has been in love for years, a prisoner, but partly too because it represents in itself a way of life that offends him deeply. When he is about to leave the Riviera, Rosemary Hoyt asks him if he is going home. "Home?" he says, "I have no home. I am going to a war," and when Rosemary asks him what war, he says, "What war? Any war. I haven't seen a paper lately but I suppose there's a war—there always is." A little shocked by this, Rosemary asks him if he doesn't care at all about what he may find himself fighting for, and he says, "Not at all— so long as I'm well treated. When I'm in a rut I come to see the Divers, because I know that in a few weeks I'll want to go to war."

The novel's central group of characters consists of Dick, Nicole, Rosemary, and these two. It is surrounded by a larger group of minor characters, each of whom shows us an aspect of the world Dick Diver lives in. There is Lady Caroline Sibley-Biers, the latest wild woman from London, petulant and stupid, whose idea of amusement is to dress up as a French sailor and pick up a girl in Antibes. There is Baby Warren, Nicole's sister, "a tall fine-looking woman deeply engaged in being thirty" who "was alien from touch" and for whom "such lingering touches as kisses and embraces slipped directly through the flesh into the forefront of her consciousness." She is supremely confident that the most dehumanized routines of British social life are the ideal existence and that her series of engagements to socially eligible Englishmen, which even she no longer really expects will come to anything, constitutes a full life. There is Albert McKisco, the confused but proud possessor of a host of secondhand ideas that safely insulate him from experience. Such characters define for us the chic grossness, the neurotic orderliness, the lifeless intellectuality of the world Dick Diver lives in. They are not what they are because they are rich, though, being rich, they are able to be what they are with a freedom and completeness that ordinary people cannot. Still, they are not what they are merely because they are rich; they are so because the world is.

In this world Dick Diver's need to reach out to people, to galvanize them into life by reminding them of the selves they originally were, is like a wound, a "lesion of vitality" as Fitzgerald calls it, from which his spiritual energy slowly drips away until there is nothing left. At the beginning of the novel, "one June morning in 1925" when Rosemary meets Dick, the first faint signs of the loss have begun to show. He is still able to produce for people such enchanted moments as the one on the beach that Rosemary has watched with delight, when he holds a whole group of people enthralled, not by what he does—what he does is almost nothing—but by the quality of his performance, the delicate sense of the tone and feeling of occasion and audience by which he can make a small group of people feel they are alone with each other in the dark universe, in some magically protected place where they can be their best selves. He performs this trick of the heart once again for Rosemary when she goes to dinner with the Divers just after she has met them. At the climax of that dinner, the table seemed just for a moment "to have risen a little toward the sky like a mechanical dancing platform" and

the two Divers began suddenly to warm and glow and expand, as if to make up to their guests, already so subtly assured of their importance, so flattered with politeness, for anything they might still miss from that country well left behind. Just for a moment they seemed to speak to every one at the table, singly and together, assuring them of their friendliness, their affection. And for a moment the faces turned up toward them were like the faces of poor children at a Christmas tree.

But now, each such moment is followed for Dick by a spell of deep melancholy in which he looks "back with awe at the carnival of affection he had given, as a general might gaze at a massacre he had ordered to satisfy an impersonal blood lust." Rosemary catches a glimpse of that melancholy, without recognizing it, her very first morning on the beach when, after all the others have gone, Dick stops to tell her she must not get too sunburned and she says with young cheerfulness, "Do you know what time it is?" and Dick says, "It's about half-past one."

They faced the seascape together momentarily.
"It's not a bad time," said Dick Diver. "It's not one of the worst times of the day."

These periods of melancholy are one consequence of his decreasing vitality; another is his inability to maintain the self-discipline he has heretofore exercised almost unconsciously because it is only by not yielding to his momentary impulses that he can fulfill his central need to make the world over for others. The first failure of this discipline—and the major one—is allowing himself to fall in love with Rosemary. Though he cannot control that impulse, he knows that it "marked a turning point in his life—it was out of line with everything that had preceded it—even out of line with what effect he might hope to produce on Rosemary." Then he finds himself drinking just a little too much in a carefully controlled way—"an ounce of gin with twice as much water" at carefully spaced intervals. The book on psychiatry he has been working on for years begins to seem to him stale and unimportant and his work at the clinic tiresome. "Not without desperation he had long felt the ethics of his profession dissolving into a lifeless mass." When Nicole has a third serious breakdown, the long months of "restating the universe for her" leave him exhausted in a way he has never known before.

He goes off alone to try to rest and get himself together and discovers to his horror that he cannot stop yielding to every vagrant impulse of his nature—to charm a pretty girl, to blurt out without regard for his listeners the bitterness in his heart. He sees more clearly than anyone what is happening to him, but since it is happening somewhere below the level of reason, beyond the control of his will, he can only watch helplessly. "He had lost himself—he could not tell the hour when, or the week, the month, or the year. . . . Between the time he found Nicole flowering under a stone on the Zurichsee and the moment of his meeting with Rosemary the spear had been blunted."

The first faint signs of this loss of self had appeared at that first meeting with Rosemary Hoyt on the beach at Antibes. When, five years later, he and Rosemary meet again on the same beach, now crowded with dull, fashionable people, he says to her, "Did you hear I'd gone into a process of deterioration? . . . It's true. The change came a long way back—but at first it didn't show. The manner remains intact after the moral cracks." By a desperate effort he can still force himself at moments to exercise that manner, but these moments come more and more rarely and require him to be drunker and drunker, a condition in which he is as likely to assert the black despair in his heart in some outburst of incoherent violence, as he does when he picks a fight in Rome with a detective and is beaten up and thrown in jail, or when at Antibes he gets into a drunken, confused argument with Lady Caroline Sibley-Biers and even she is able to make him look foolish. These scenes are almost intolerably moving, for Fitzgerald's lifelong habit of giving events the value they have for the person who suffers them rather than their conventional public value makes us feel these trivial misfortunes as what they are, the loose ends of life, as Zelda once said, with which men hang themselves.

Finally Dick accepts the exhaustion of his vitality and its consequences, his inability to control himself to any purpose, his inability to love and be loved by others. He sets himself to cut his losses—his responsibilities for Nicole and the children and his friends—and to bury his dead—himself. The task is made simpler by the fact that Nicole has now recovered completely. Though she still depends on Dick, her dependence is now only old habit, not necessity. As she has recovered she has become more and more the superficially orderly, inwardly anarchic barbarian that has always been her true Warren self. As such, she turns instinctively away from Dick and toward Tommy Barban. Dick therefore sets himself to break her dependence on him and to push her toward Tommy. At the last moment he deliberately provokes a quarrel with her and then watches silently while she struggles to deny him and assert her independence. When she succeeds, "Dick waited until she was out of sight. Then he leaned his head forward on the parapet. The case was finished. Doctor Diver was at liberty."

Dick stays at Antibes just long enough to make sure Nicole is safe in Tommy's hands and then leaves for America, taking with him nothing, least of all himself.

Nicole kept in touch with Dick after her marriage [to Tommy]. . . . [He] opened an office in Buffalo, but evidently without success. Nicole did not find what the trouble was, but she heard a few months later that he was in a little town named Batavia, New York, practicing general medicine, and later that he was in Lockport, doing the same thing. . . . He was considered to have fine manners and once made a good speech at a public health meeting on the subject of drugs; but he became entangled with a girl who worked in a grocery store, and he was involved in a law suit about some medical question; so he left Lockport. After that he didn't ask for the children to be sent to America and didn't answer when Nicole wrote asking him if he needed money. . . . His latest note was post-marked from Hornell, New York, which is some distance from Geneva and a small town; in any case he is certainly in that section of the country, in one town or another.

ERNEST HEMINGWAY
1898-1961

The Sun Also Rises
1926

Ernest Hemingway was three years younger than Scott Fitzgerald, though *The Sun Also Rises,* his first novel, was written eight years before *Tender Is the Night,* Fitzgerald's last. Hemingway and Fitzgerald were close friends, as close as two such high-strung "romantic egotists" could be. There were plenty of troubles between them, and when they were together it was always touch-and-go whether they would quarrel or not. But there was also between them an admiration and an affection that survived everything. When Hemingway emerged as a writer, Fitzgerald already had a considerable reputation and used it enthusiastically in his advocacy of Hemingway's work. He bombarded Max Perkins, his editor at Scribner's, with praise of Hemingway and made a habit of bullying other writers to join the crusade, telling them he thought they would agree that *The Great Gatsby* (then just published) and their latest books "were rather inflated market values," and pressing them to say what they would do to help launch Hemingway; and "now and then [he] impatiently grasped and shook [their] elbow[s]." "It simply had not occurred to him," as Glenway Wescott—one of his victims—observed, "that unfriendliness or pettiness on my part might inhibit my enthusiasm about the art of a new colleague and rival." At the same time Hemingway was trusting Fitzgerald's judgment—in the plotting to get Scribner's to take Hemingway on—further than he was ever again to trust another man's.

Six months before Fitzgerald died, after there had been such difficulties between them that Fitzgerald could not write Hemingway directly, he was anxiously asking Max Perkins, "How does Ernest feel about things? . . . I would be interested in at least a clue to Ernest's attitude"; and after Fitzgerald died, Hemingway said quite simply, "I loved Scott very much [though] he was extremely difficult. . . ." Beneath all the differences of personality and conscious commitment, there was a similarity of values and a distinction of talent that each could feel in the other. They were alike also in being—though in different ways—men of their time, and the values of both had a special validity for their age. Philip Young has put this point very well about Hemingway. *"The Sun Also Rises,"* he says, "touched with delicate accuracy on something big, on things other people were feeling, but too dimly for articulation. Hemingway had deeply felt and understood what was in the wind." *The Sun Also Rises* belongs to that class of books like Etherege's *Man of Mode* (which is what its hero, Jake Barnes, is for his age) that, with superb honesty, catches the attitude of a period and, by doing so before that attitude has clearly defined itself, helps to create it.

The clear scorn in *The Sun Also Rises* for the clichés widespread among the fashionable intellectuals of the time shows how deeply Hemingway believed he had penetrated to the reality of the human situation in his time. "Don't eat that, Lady—that's Mencken," as Bill Gorton says. It is largely Bill Gorton who makes this point for Hemingway (because Jake Barnes, who is narrator as well as hero, could not). Bill makes fun of the age's preoccupation with irony and pity by pointing out how little of either Jake has. "They're mad about [irony and pity] in New York," he tells Jake. "It's just like the Fratellinis used to be." (That comparison is acute. There was a cult of the popular arts—"the seven lively arts"—in New York in the twenties. One was not abreast of the times if he was not enthusiastically knowledgeable about Charlie Chaplin, Archy and Mehitabel, and circus performers like the Fratellinis; Hart Crane wrote a serious poem about Chaplin, "Chaplinesque.")

Bill Gorton produces a wonderful parody of the stock attitude of New York intellectuals toward writers like Jake. It is a mixture of Van Wyck Brooks's intellectualized provincialism and the sentimental Dorothy Parker irony-and-pity that found in Chaplin its ideal hero. Bill says to Jake:

"You claim you want to be a writer, too. You're only a newspaper man. An expatriate newspaper man. You ought to be ironical the minute you get out of bed. You ought to wake up with your mouth full of pity. . . . Why don't you live in New York? Then you'd know these things. . . . You know what's the trouble with you? You're an expatriate. One of the worst types. . . . Nobody that ever left their own country ever wrote anything worth printing. . . . You've lost touch with the soil. You get precious. Fake European standards have ruined you. You drink yourself to death. You become obsessed by sex. You spend all your time talking, not working. You're an expatriate, see? You hang around cafés."

To this, Jake, who lives a disciplined, hard-working life by which he earns those pleasures that express his deepest emotions, can rightly say, "It sounds like a swell life. When do I work?"

Thus Hemingway demonstrates the falseness of the New York intellectual's analysis of those who really understand the life of their times and know the ethical imperatives it imposes. But Jake's own understanding of experience is, in a more serious and responsible way, also a shared one. Hemingway believed he was seeing life entirely for himself. Insofar as that meant he accepted as true only what was borne out by his personal experience, he was right; but insofar as it meant he had discovered his truth for himself, in his own unique experience, he was not right. Like the New York intellectuals he satirizes, Hemingway took much of what he believed about experience from the air around him, the mood of his age. The difference was that he chose with much greater insight, and accepted only what rang true for his own feelings; but often what rang true did so simply because his feelings were themselves products of his time. It is an important part of Hemingway's value as a writer that this was so. His relentless determination to feel for himself everything he accepted makes his work genuine. The familiarity of much of what he felt—what Gertrude Stein scornfully called the bourgeois quality of his nature—made his work representative. To speak with all the eloquence of his deepest feelings Hemingway did not, happily, have to say something novel, eccentric, invalid for everyone but himself. He could in all sincerity speak for his time—for the best of his time—so that Bill Gorton's Lady can still eat him safely, as she cannot Mencken or Burton Rascoe.

The Sun Also Rises thus expresses something that not only was important in its own time but also is valuable in ours, both because it is interesting as cultural history and because any view of experience actually lived out by an age has, when it is deeply felt and fully expressed in an image of its age, permanent value. Hemingway's age was, for all its ostensible pessimism, an energetic one that believed in the possibility of happiness even if it often represented that possibility as defeated by life. One result of that is that Hemingway's work (and Fitzgerald's too) has taken on for later generations the glamor of romance. "There is," as Philip Young quite rightly says, "a gaping cleavage [in *The Sun Also Rises*] between manner and message, between joy in life and a pronouncement of life's futility . . . and one's net impression today is of all the fun there is to be had in getting good and lost." *The Sun Also Rises* has become—as Fitzgerald noticed—"a romance and a guidebook." But its interest both as cultural history and as a model of the good life for aging undergraduates along the Left Bank is a by-product of its greatness.

That greatness consists in the purity, the cleanness, the sharpness of definition with which Hemingway embodies in action what he felt to be the truth about experience. That truth has its limitations; they are set both by the limits of Hemingway's time and by the limits of his own nature. But it is not so simple as people have sometimes thought, though in his anxiety to include nothing he did not truly feel—nothing secondhand—Hemingway often unintentionally encourages people to think him a naïf. But whatever one's judgment of the paraphrasable "philosophical" content of Hemingway's work, that judgment does not define its value. Its value is that what his work implies about experience, whatever its limitations, is something Hemingway has known, not as idea learned, but as experience felt. What a man knows in this way has its own important kind of truth, and it is worth reminding ourselves how precious such truth is: most men have little capacity for any of it. Moreover, Hemingway had the talent to communicate to us what he did know exactly as he knew it— the way, as he himself once put it, it was.

"A writer's job," he said, "is to tell the truth," and to tell the truth, as Hemingway understood the word, is enormously difficult. It is difficult to know this truth, to clear away all secondhand opinions and habits of feeling and to expose to one's own understanding what one does feel. It is even more difficult to say what that is after one has unearthed it, since words are always cluttered with the blurred, commonplace feelings of a society's routine assumptions about the meaning of experience. Hemingway certainly often felt, as did Frederic Henry of *A Farewell to Arms,* that "there were many words that you could not stand to hear and finally only the names of places had dignity." He always felt that the simple words—the ones that carried the smallest burden of stock attitudes—were the safest ones. Moreover, he was sure that all abstract ideas about experience—not just the commonplace ones—were falsifying. At best they are paraphrases of the real thing, of the feelings with which one responds to experience directly; at worst they are a simplified model of experience that people fix on as if it were reality and thus lose their capacity to respond to experience itself. This habit is the main trouble with Robert Cohn in *The Sun Also Rises,* and its consequences are disastrous. "The funny thing is he's nice, too. I like him," as Bill Gorton says. "But he's just so awful." All men, but specially novelists, should avoid abstract ideas. "In five years," as Jake Barnes tells himself, "[each such idea] will seem just as silly as all the other fine philosophies I've had."

What you must respond to are things and experiences themselves, not ideas about them, and the closer you stick to them, the less risk there is that you will lose what you truly feel about them under a midden of abstractions. Hemingway's style—both in the narrow sense of the kinds of words he limits himself to and in the larger sense of the kinds of things he selects to talk about—is a triumph, the isolation of exactly the means this purpose requires. "No matter how good a phrase or a simile [a writer] may have," he said, "if he puts it in where it is not absolutely necessary and irreplaceable he is spoiling his work for egotism. Prose is architecture, not interior decoration, and the Baroque is over." So, at least, it was for Hemingway.

This is the reason Hemingway was determined to write down only the actual things he had seen and heard and the actual experiences he had lived, in words that would be as close to the actual thing, as little decorated with meanings not part of his immediate experience, as possible. In this sense he was a great realist. But what he selected from actual experience was not selected for its own sake, for some value intrinsic to it. What he selected was chosen because he had *felt* something significant about it, something that constituted a part of what he calls the truth. In this sense, he was a great impressionist.

The principle on which Hemingway selected and arranged the particulars of his fiction has some resemblance to the principle worked out by Ezra Pound and made famous by T. S. Eliot as the doctrine of the objective correlative: the particulars that constitute a fiction must, on this principle, be so selected as to evoke in the reader a "curve of feeling." Hemingway's idea differs from Pound's and Eliot's mainly in his commitment to choosing the particulars he uses from among those that actually caused him to feel the emotions he is trying, in the story, to evoke from the reader. Pound and Eliot saw no need for this. Pound does not even mention the particulars that cause the poet to have his emotion: "some very vivid and undeniable adventure," he calls them; nor does he specify the kind of particulars that will constitute the objective correlative, or what he calls "the myth"; he simply says the writer produces "an impersonal or objective story woven out of his own emotions." Eliot does not mention the occasion that generates the emotion at all; he goes straight to how it must be expressed: "The only way of expressing emotion in art is by finding an 'objective correlative'; in other words, a set of objects, a situation, a chain of events which shall be the formula of that *particular* emotion; such that when the external facts, which must terminate in sensory experience, are given, the emotion is immediately evoked." Clearly, in this view, there need be no relation between the actual occasion that created the emotion in the poet and the fictional occasion constructed by the poet to evoke this emotion in the reader. The fictional occasion may be of any kind. The important thing is to define exactly the emotion one is trying to evoke ("the formula of that *particular* emotion").

This is not an insignificant difference; it means that Hemingway is a realist and Pound and Eliot are not. Nevertheless the fundamental purpose of a fiction—to evoke a particular emotion—and its means— a set of carefully selected concrete particulars—are the same for both. (This theory of literature has dominated the twentieth century; whether it is true or not may be a question.)

One can see the way Hemingway was committed to this theory in his account of how he worked to make himself a writer. "I found," he says, "the greatest difficulty, aside from knowing truly what you really felt, rather than what you were supposed to feel, and had been taught to feel, was to put down what really happened in action; what the actual things were that produced the emotions." The whole theory is implied there. The story must consist of "actual things"; these things are selected from the totality of the actual because precisely they "produced the emotions" that you experienced and—it is assumed—will evoke them in the reader. The main problem is to define the emotions exactly, and the way to do so is to identify the "actual things . . . that produced the emotions." Real emotions are the products of actual experience; they can never be had secondhand, by reading books or hearing about them and imagining you have felt them, as Robert Cohn does when he reads *The Purple Land* or remembers what he has been told at Princeton about Gothic cathedrals. This is the point Hemingway is making when Jake says to Robert about Robert's yearning to go to South America, "You can see all the South Americans you want in Paris anyway." Confidently confusing what he has imagined from reading *The Purple Land* with real experience, Robert says, "They're not real South Americans." "They look awfully real to me," Jake says.

"Chaps," as Brett says, "never know anything" until they have lived through it—and only then, of course, when they are aware of exactly what it is all about and have some natural capacity for emotions. "But of course," as Eliot once put it, "only those who have personality and emotions" know what it means to suffer from them. It follows for Hemingway—as a principle of conduct rather than of art—that feelings must issue in actual experience, must be expressed in action, if they are to achieve definition. "Love's mysteries in souls do grow,/ But yet the body is his book," as John Donne, a poet Hemingway much admired, said. In fact, the proper use of sensory experience is the realization of emotion. An emotion unrealized is not truly known, not what its possessor imagines it is, like the emotion of the young bride in the A. E. W. Mason story Jake reads during the fishing trip. Her husband had fallen into a glacier, and she was—all passion unspent—"going to wait twenty-four years exactly for his body to come out on the moraine, while her true love waited too." That last phrase shows us what we are to think of this program.

For the same reason sensory experience indulged in for its own sake, without emotion or in the service of a falsely conceived emotion, is bad. In short, sensory experience is the language of emotion, whether it be the pleasure of being in beautiful country like rural Spain or fine cities like Paris, or of watching or performing exercises of disciplined skill like hunting, bullfighting, or dancing, or of eating and drinking, or of sex. Only when you truly love are these pleasures

K

of the senses real, and only when it issues in sensory experience does your love take its true form. "Afterward, all that was faked [by a bullfighter] turned bad and gave an unpleasant feeling. Romero's bullfighting gave real emotion, because he kept absolute purity of line in his movements and always quietly and calmly let the horns pass him close each time." "And calmly let the horns pass him close each time," for the occasions of the most significant emotions are those of death and love. That is why the bullfighter lives his life all the way up: he faces death with the disciplined grace of a ballet dancer. That is why the injury that makes the realization of love impossible for Jake is so difficult for him to accept; it deprives him of the only great occasion for emotion he has the gift for.

Hemingway focuses on this point in "The Short, Happy Life of Francis Macomber," when Francis achieves maturity by facing death with a calm exercise of skill and suddenly finds his life has a meaning he had never even imagined before. The inevitable result is that he finds intolerable the beautiful but quite unchanged woman he had chosen before this change occurred. Even the inexpert amateur, like the man who runs before the bulls during the *encierro,* has caught a glimpse of the great life. That is what makes stupid the ostensible common sense of the waiter at the Iruna who says, when one of these men is gored, "Badly cogido through the back. . . . A big horn wound. All for fun. Just for fun. What do you think of that?" "You're not an aficionado?" Jake asks. "Me?" says the waiter. "What are bulls? Animals. Brute animals." The "unpleasant feeling" you have after watching a bullfighter who fakes tells you the act has not been the true expression of real emotion. The same thing is true in human relations. Jake found that he "liked to see [Mike Campbell] hurt Cohn. I wished he would not do it, though, because afterwards it made me disgusted at myself. That was morality; things that made you disgusted afterwards. No, that must be immorality."

You must see very precisely what actually happens if you are to have the moral guidance of feelings like these. Some people, like Brett, have a natural gift for doing so; otherwise you must learn. When you do, when you love the thing and thoroughly understand the craft of its performance, then the thing itself may be, by conventional standards, quite insignificant. When Jake is on the fishing trip with Bill Gorton, he wakes in the night and hears the cold wind blowing and is happy: "It felt good to be warm and in bed." When he walks to his office in Paris early on a fine morning he knows a similar happiness.

In the morning I walked down the Boulevard to the rue Soufflot for coffee and brioche. It was a fine morning. The horse-chestnut trees in the Luxembourg gardens were in bloom. There was the pleasant early-morning feeling of a hot day. I read the papers with the coffee and then smoked a cigarette. . . . All along people were going to work. It felt pleasant to be going to work. I walked across the avenue and turned into my office.

For a romantic of Hemingway's kind, then, what T. E. Hulme called the divine—that is, the ideal condition—is life, however ordinary, at its intensest. Hemingway was perfectly consistent when, shortly before he killed himself, he told Mr. Hotchner that there was no point in living when you were no longer capable of sensory experience—not because sensory experience is in itself the purpose of existence but because it is the only way men can know the love that is.

These pleasures have to be earned, by a precise understanding of the things you love and by the good behavior that frees you to love them. "You paid for everything that was any good . . ." Jake thinks. "Either you paid by learning, . . . or by experience, or by taking chances, or by money. Enjoying living was learning to get your money's worth and knowing when you had it." Not that such enjoyment is always possible. Much of the time "they" make it impossible. "You did not know what it was about. You never had time to learn," as Frederic Henry thinks. "They threw you in and told you the rules and the first time they caught you off base they killed you. . . . You could count on that. Stay around and they would kill you." Still, you know what the true joy of living is, whether "they" allow you to have it or not: it is realized love. Whatever the limitations of this idea, abstractly considered, Hemingway was able to make an image for it in *The Sun Also Rises* that is truly felt and magnificently expressed; this is the novel's greatness.

Its outward form, its story, is slight. It covers a few weeks of the spring in Paris during which we watch Jake Barnes living his customary life, a fishing trip in Spain and the week of the fiesta in Pamplona that follows, and a few days after the fiesta. Running through this small slice of Jake Barnes's life is a minimal plot, the working out of the relation between Jake Barnes and Brett, with whom Jake has been in love off and on for a long time now. But when the novel ends, Jake and Brett are exactly where they were at the start. It cannot even be said that they understand their situation better or are better reconciled to it, for they knew all there was to know about it at the start. The novel ends where it began. The first serious remark Brett makes, on the first occasion when we see her and Jake together, is, "Oh, darling. I've been so miserable"; and the last thing she says in the book is, "Oh, Jake, we could have had such a damned good time together"—and Jake says, "Yes. Isn't it pretty to think so?" "Pretty," the derogatory term, because thinking it is bad. We have been, throughout the novel, circling about on the same spot, and when we have returned to the point on the circle at which we began, the novel ends. "I see a crowd of people, walking round in a ring," as *The Waste Land* says.

The novel's meaning is not in a plot, then, or in any development of a character, except as it is part of its meaning that the essential conditions of life do not change and that "you can't," as Fitzgerald's Dick Diver says, "do anything about people." The meaning of the novel is in the conduct of characters caught in a situation they cannot get out of, conduct that gradually reveals the differences between behaving well and behaving badly. The right thing for men to do is to recognize their situation for exactly what it is and to learn to accept it, and the only way for them to act is to behave well in that situation, to show—as Hemingway once put it—grace under pressure. The situation is sure to put pressure on everyone, and even the best will occasionally crack under it, at least in private. "I try," says Jake as he lies on his bed in the dark thinking about Brett,

> I try and play along and just not make trouble for people. Probably I never would have had any trouble if I hadn't run into Brett when they shipped me to England. I suppose she only wanted what she couldn't have [just as he does]. . . . Then . . . I was thinking about Brett and my mind stopped jumping around and started to go in sort of smooth waves. Then all of a sudden I started to cry. . . . It is awfully easy to be hard-boiled about everything in the daytime, but at night it is another thing.

Jake has tried any number of remedies for this trouble; he even tries keeping the light on all night ("After all," as the old waiter in "A Clean, Well-Lighted Place" says, "it is probably only insomnia. Many must have it"). But one cannot—as Jake recalls the Catholic Church advises—stop thinking about what one cannot have. All one can do is to prevent oneself from behaving badly and making trouble for people when one is, as Bill Gorton puts it, "a little daunted." Then, like Harvey Stone, one "goes off like a cat," by oneself. Most people cannot even do that. When, for example, Brett falls violently in love with Romero, she cannot stop herself from seducing him, though she knows she is behaving badly, making trouble for Romero and a good many other people—notably Jake and Mike Campbell. "I can't help it," she says honestly. "I've never been able to help anything."

Thus the novel establishes a double set of criteria for judging people. The first question to be asked is: is he "one of us"; that is, is he one of those who have learned to understand what the circumstances of their existence really are and what they truly feel? Those who have done so recognize one another at once, as Brett recognizes that Count Mippipopolous is "quite one of us," although he is a fat Greek who has made a fortune in America from a chain of candy stores and wears an Elk's tooth on his watch chain. But he knows that "you don't mix emotions with [a superb champagne]. You lose the taste," and he has no interest in knowledge for its own sake: he wants it only to focus sensation and define emotion; when Jake says casually that he ought to write a book about wines, he says, "Mr. Barnes, all I want out of wines is to enjoy them."

These people who know what life really is constitute an inner group in the novel, almost a secret society of those with *afición,* the true passion. They may have nothing else in common, as Jake and the Pamplona hotel owner, Montoya, have nothing in common but their passion for bullfighting. It is enough. "We never talked for a long time. It was simply the pleasure of discovering what we each felt. Men would come from distant towns and before they left Pamplona stop and talk for a few minutes with Montoya about bulls. These men were aficionados."

But being one of us is not enough; there is also the question of how you behave. "I did not care what it was all about," Jake thinks. "All I wanted to know was how to live in it." First, that is, you must really live in it; second, you must live in it well, with dignity. "Maybe if you found out how to live in it you learned from that what it was all about." Certainly you would never learn what it was all about any other way. This second criterion—how well you behave—does not of course apply to those who are not one of us; such people either behave in a harmless but quite irrelevant way—as do the nice but hopelessly unaware pair from Montana whom Jake and Bill meet on the train to Bayonne—or in a sincerely self-righteous and self-pitying way that makes a great deal of trouble for other people, as does Cohn's mistress, Francis Clyne. This second criterion is applicable only to those who know what life is, the inner group of the novel's characters. With these it is necessary to distinguish between those who behave well no matter how much pressure the situation puts on them —as do Bill Gorton, who is only lightly tried, and Jake, who is heavily tried—and those who behave badly, as do Brett and Mike, both of whom are heavily tried.

The essential purpose of the novel's design is to give the maximum immediacy, the most intense and particularized dramatic life, to these distinctions among the characters. Its form is, like the form of so many twentieth-century fictions, more significantly spatial than linear, more like a picture in which the significant aspects of the characters' natures are brought out by the grouping than like a narrative that moves in a significant way through time to a decisive conclusion. What has to be watched closely is this grouping, not the development of the plot.

At the novel's center are Jake and Brett. Jake has been wounded in the war in such a way that—though not castrated and deprived of sexual response like a steer (Robert Cohn is like a steer: he is emotionally castrated)—he is incapable of sexual intercourse. This fact is not so much a symbol, in the usual sense, of the condition in which the war has left men (and, by extension, the condition in which life usually leaves men who understand it) as it is a real instance of the condition of such men. For Hemingway literature as well as life has no meaning, no general "philosophy," independent of immediate experience that can be symbolized by a thought-out set of objects. Jake's injury is a representative but literal instance of the tricks "they" play on men, a real example of the kind of thing men must contend with.

In both Brett and Jake, the emotion of love seeks its natural and proper issue in sexual intercourse, which, because of Jake's injury, is impossible. When they run into each other at the *bal musette* they are for a moment happy: they are deeply in love and have missed one another badly. Brett has been rushing about but has been "miserable"; Jake has been so bored that he has picked up a *poule* to have dinner with. For a moment just being together is enough for them; "we were dancing to the accordion and some one was playing the banjo. I was hot and I felt happy." But this happiness leads them naturally to go off together, and when they get into the taxi and Jake kisses Brett, they face once more the terrible frustration of love's proper expression. Because Brett turns "to jelly when you touch me," she cannot bear to have him do so. But they cannot keep apart and so avoid this moment either. "But, darling," as Brett says, "I have to see you. It isn't all that you know." But it cannot, just the same, rightly exist without "that." In a moment of weakness Jake says, "Couldn't we live together, Brett? Couldn't we just live together?" But Brett says, "I don't think so. I'd just *tromper* you with everybody. You couldn't stand it." They both know that is true.

Around this central pair of characters Hemingway groups a set of minor ones. Each of them is carefully placed by the action, first, according to whether he is one of us, and second, if he is, according to how well he behaves. Directly over against Jake is Robert Cohn. Cohn begins as a modest naïf. He is not one of us, but in his unpretentious innocence he is nice. Then he goes to New York, where he has a book accepted and wins money at cards. After that "he talked several times of how a man could always make a living at bridge if he were forced to" and began to be "not so simple and not so nice." In his newfound self-confidence he also begins to work up a number of ideas about how to live, mostly borrowed from books, and becomes "not so pleasant to have around." Cohn worries that his "life is going so fast and I'm not really living it." Out of his own hard-earned wisdom Jake says to him, "Nobody ever lives their life all the way up except bull-fighters." No one, that is, has the bullfighter's purity of passion and—if he is skillful and brave enough—his opportunity to realize that passion completely in disciplined action. Everybody else must recognize the life he has for what it is and live in it as fully as he can. Robert Cohn is hopelessly incapable of understanding any of this. "I'm not interested in bull-fighters," he says. "That's an abnormal life."

Then this newly assured Cohn meets Brett. "He looked a great deal as his compatriot must have looked when he saw the promised land. Cohn, of course, was much younger. But he had that look of eager, deserving expectation." It never occurs to Cohn to wonder what Jake's feelings about Brett may be because he is wholly taken up with his own bookish feelings for Brett.

"There's a certain quality about her," he says, "a certain fineness. She seems to be absolutely fine and straight."

"She's very nice," Jake says.

"I don't know how to describe the quality. I suppose it's breeding. . . . I shouldn't wonder if I were in love with her."

"She's a drunk," Jake says. "She's in love with Mike Campbell, and she's going to marry him. He's going to be rich as hell some day."

When Cohn says Brett "must have been just a kid" when Jake met her during the war, Jake says, "She's thirty-four," and when Cohn says, "I don't believe she would marry anybody she didn't love," Jake says, "Well, she's done it twice." Jake loves Brett very much, but what he loves is Brett as she actually is, not some literary idea of what she ought to be. Cohn loves an idea of Brett that suits the self-regarding dream of life he has worked up for himself. "He calls her Circe," Mike Campbell says. "He claims she turns men into swine. Damn good. I wish I were one of these literary chaps."

Then Brett goes off for a weekend with Cohn, out of boredom and a desire to get away from the pain of constantly seeing Jake. Like the other casual affairs Brett has, this is an immoral act, sex used as an anodyne for boredom, not as an expression of love. ("What shall I do now? What shall I do?/ I shall rush out as I am, and walk the street/ With my hair down, so. What shall we do tomorrow?/ What shall we ever do?") Brett's going off with Cohn proves what Jake had implied about her in his conversation with Cohn, that, though one of us, she behaves badly. But to Cohn it proves he is her own true love. This weekend occurs just before the three of them, together with Jake's friend Bill Gorton and Brett's fiancé, Mike Campbell, are to meet at Pamplona for the week of the fiesta. Jake and Bill join Robert at Bayonne to drive to Pamplona (Mike and Brett are to follow). In Bayonne they take a look at the cathedral. "Cohn [remembering something from an art course at Princeton] made some remark about it being a good example of something or other, I forget what. It seemed [to Jake, who knows only what he truly feels] a nice cathedral, nice and dim, like Spanish churches." Then they drive into the magnificent Spanish countryside. Jake "was up in front with the driver and turned around. Robert Cohn was asleep, but Bill looked and nodded his head."

When they reach Pamplona, Jake goes to the cathedral and tries to pray, but without much success. "I was a little ashamed, and regretted that I was such a rotten Catholic, but realized there was nothing I could do about it. . . . I only wished I felt religious . . ." But nobody knows better than he how far that is from actually feeling religious. "And then I was out in the hot sun on the steps of the cathedral, and the forefinger and the thumb of my right hand were still damp, and I felt them dry in the sun." And that minutely specific sensation—with its suggestion of the whole quality of being in Spain and having the fiesta—he knows is real. Meanwhile Cohn is displaying an irritating complacency about Brett and rushing about having his hair cut, as if he was sure Brett could not wait to see him again. Cohn's behavior is silly enough; just the same, he has possessed Brett as Jake never can, and his air of the successful lover is a constant reminder to Jake. "I was blind, unforgiving jealous of what had happened to him. The fact that I took it as a matter of course [that is, that he behaved well about it] did not alter that any."

Mike Campbell, on the other hand, behaves badly about the airs Cohn puts on. He turns out to be a bad drunk, and when he is drunk he will say to Cohn, "Why don't you say something, Robert? Don't sit there looking like a bloody funeral. What if Brett did sleep with you? She's slept with lots of better people than you." "I don't like Cohn, God knows," as Bill Gorton puts it, ". . . but nobody has any business to talk like Mike." Mike behaves equally badly when Brett takes up with Romero.

Besides behaving badly about Brett, Mike is a bankrupt. This reminds us that among other things Jake says you must pay for the good things of life is money. ("Either you paid by learning about them, or by experience, or by taking chances, or by money.") It is not that money can buy the emotion, the capacity to love truly that is the essential thing. About the economy of the emotions Hemingway was very much a classical economist: he believed in individual initiative and hard work. There is a passage near the end of *The Sun Also Rises* that shows his attitude clearly. Exhausted by the strain of real emotions exercised in an actual situation that he has experienced for a week at the fiesta in Spain, Jake feels ironic relief at finding himself back in the different atmosphere of France. The atmosphere of France is a release from pain, but at the cost, of course, of not being serious, as life in Spain is.

> Everything is on a clear financial basis in France. . . . No one makes things complicated by becoming your friend for any obscure reason. If you want people to like you you have only to spend a little money [for Americans in France, Fitzgerald said, "the snow of twenty-nine wasn't real snow. If you didn't want it to be snow, you just paid some money"]. I spent a little money and the waiter liked me. He appreciated my valuable qualities. . . . It [was] a sincere liking because it [had] a sound basis. I was back in France.

But if you cannot buy life, paying your debts is nevertheless, like honoring any other obligation acquired in the course of living, an important part of behaving well, and Mike Campbell never pays his debts.

Like Brett, Mike is one of us, and he is, like her, completely honest about himself. By being so he manages to make a very funny story out of how he gave away a lot of medals in a nightclub. "Gave one to each girl," he says. "Form of souvenir. They thought I was hell's own shakes of a soldier. Give away medals in a nightclub. Dashing fellow." But, like Brett again, Mike has "never been able to help anything" about himself, has never been able to stop himself from doing what he cannot pay for. He had borrowed those medals with no more thought of returning them than he had of paying his tailor's bill. He says so quite frankly. "Seems some chap had left [these medals with his tailor] to be cleaned. . . . Set hell's own store by them. . . . Rotten luck for the tailor." He is equally honest about the fact that he is not

at all a dashing fellow. He fights Robert Cohn when Cohn insults
Jake, and he gets knocked down, but he does not pretend to like it.
"He didn't knock me out [he had knocked Jake out]," Mike says.
"I just lay there. . . . I'm not one of those chaps who likes being
knocked about. I never play games even. . . . I never liked to hunt,
you know. There was always the danger of having the horse fall on
you." Mike has the same kind of realism about the way he lives—and
the dignity of that realism—that the *poule,* Georgette, has when she
stands up to the malice of Mrs. Braddocks and the *patronne*'s daughter. But neither behaves well.

Mike borrows money from Montoya without intending to repay it
("The hell you did," Jake says); he pays his hotel bill with Brett's
money; he rents a car to go to Bayonne without having money to pay
for it; he gambles without being able to pay his "debts of honor"
(when he says so, "Bill's face sort of changed"). When the people
who had once bailed out him and Brett at Cannes and had never, of
course, been repaid were rude to Mike, Bill said, "No one ought to
have the right to say things about Mike. . . . I wish to hell they didn't
have any right." But they do.

In his different way Cohn behaves as badly as Mike. "Somehow he
seemed to enjoy [being insulted by Mike]. The childish, drunken
heroics of it. It was his affair with a lady of title." Brett does her best
to shut Mike up and to prevent Cohn's following her about with his
soulful look, like some high-school Lancelot, at once cringing and
complacent. "Was I rude enough to him?" she says to Jake. "My God!
I'm so sick of him." "He's behaved very badly," Jake says. "And
Michael," Brett adds. "Michael's been lovely, too." But Mike is not
Cohn, and Jake says, "It's been damned hard on Mike" (but not, we
are to remember, so hard as it has been on Jake). "Yes," says Brett,
but she sticks to her point. "But he didn't need to be a swine." "Everybody behaves badly," Jake says. "Give them a proper chance." "You
wouldn't behave badly," Brett says.

Nor does he behave badly, about her. In his more realistic way, in
fact, he makes for Brett the gallant, ideal-lover's gesture Robert Cohn

imagines he is making when it comes his turn to be jealous of Romero, as Jake had earlier been of him. Jake had taken his jealousy "as a matter of course." Cohn persuades himself that, as Brett's true love, he is duty-bound to protect her and, thus self-deceived, is able to indulge his jealousy by beating everyone up. Romero defeats him by refusing to adopt Cohn's schoolboy code and cry quits; "he said if Cohn helped him [to get up] he'd kill him. . . ." After he has treated himself to slugging everyone, Cohn begs Jake to forgive him on the score that everyone ought to feel sorry for him ("I've been through hell, Jake. It's been simply hell")—as if it were possible to forgive him, not the beating itself, but the impossible attitude it expressed. What Cohn imagined he was being to Brett, her knightly lover, Jake really is, but because the true Brett is no Guinevere but an all-too-ordinary woman, what he has to do for her is anything but pretty; it is only what she really wants done.

Early in the novel Montoya and Jake agree that for a young and dedicated bullfighter like Romero to get mixed up with sophisticated, cosmopolitan women would be disastrous. But when Brett wants Romero, it is Jake she asks to introduce her to him. He does so, and then leaves them together; "the hard-eyed people at the bull-fighter table watched me go." It is not very pleasant for him; he has come very close to pandering for Brett, understanding as well as anyone the harm that can come to Romero, knowing that Brett's happiness with Romero will be twice as hard to endure as her meaningless affair with Cohn. But he has to choose between doing what Brett wants and what his love of bullfighting requires, and he chooses to do his lady's will, however much it pains him.

Brett quickly decides to give up Romero. "I'm not going to be one of those bitches that ruins children," she says (Brett is thirty-four, Romero nineteen). She has behaved badly; now she means to behave well. "You know," she says to Jake in one of Hemingway's rare flawed expressions of his ethic (flawed, perhaps, because it is too literally true to fact), "it makes one feel good deciding not to be a bitch. . . . It's sort of what we have instead of God." ("That was morality, things that made you disgusted afterward. No, that must be immorality.") But of course she is broke when she decides to leave Romero: it had taken all her own money to pay the bill at Pamplona and she will not take Romero's money. So she sends for Jake: "COULD YOU COME TO HOTEL MONTANA MADRID AM RATHER IN TROUBLE." These are the conditions of Jake's life, the conditions in which he must behave well if he can. He sees better than anyone the humiliation of his position but if he is to behave well as Brett's lover, he must accept that humiliation. "That was it," he thinks. "Send a girl off with one man. Introduce her to another to go off with him. Now go and bring her back. And sign the wire with love. That was it all right."

The difference between the values shown by the conduct of Jake Barnes, the twenties' true man of mode, and of Robert Cohn, the twenties' Sir Fopling Flutter, is not that Cohn is a romantic and Jake Barnes not. They are both romantics. But Cohn is falsely so: his values are secondhand; they are maintained by a "literary" distortion of the actual conditions of his life; and they encourage an egotistical disregard of the interests of others, even of his beloved. Jake's values are earned: they have been felt in his actual experience; they depend on an undistorted view of the actual conditions of life; and they encourage him to behave with consideration for others, above all his beloved, even when she requires him to behave shamefully. This basic contrast of the book is refined in all sorts of ways by the minor characters, each of whom is a variation on either Jake or Cohn, and the whole pattern is set forth in a lively representation of the manners of Hemingway's age.

In *The Sun Also Rises* Hemingway came close to the ideal Henry James once described as putting "all that is possible of one's idea into a form and compass that will contain and express it only by delicate adjustments and an exquisite chemistry, so that there will at the end be neither a drop of one's liquor left nor a hair's breadth of one's glass to spare"; and the form he created is a brilliant representation of his age. *The Sun Also Rises* is the supreme realistic image of the romantic attitude toward private experience as it existed in the twenties, perhaps the last period of American society in which the private life was still lived in the public world.

WILLIAM FAULKNER
1897-1962

The Sound and the Fury

1929

William Faulkner was unquestionably the greatest American novelist of the twentieth century, and it is unfortunate that, despite his fame, the very real difficulty of his books has prevented a great many people from reading them. Like Dickens in the nineteenth century, Faulkner was one of those rare writers who are something more than novelists. The design of many of his books has an almost Joycean sophistication and that may suggest that his imagination has too; but in fact it was much more like the imaginations to be found in the great anonymous folktales and ballads. Like their authors—and like Dickens—Faulkner loved plots in which he worked out with great ingenuity an immense number of grotesque and arbitrary complications; he delighted in the most outlandish characters; he had a passion for genealogy that would have done credit to the author of *Beowulf;* and he was completely unashamed of the kind of theatrical rhetoric that sophisticated writers are supposed to think tasteless.

It was undoubtedly an advantage for Faulkner that he was born in Mississippi, in the heart of the deep South. It may be that the brilliant group of literary critics who have come out of the South in this century have made us believe more than we should in the unique advantages for writers of being Southerners. Certainly they have done as good a public-relations job for the culture of the South as more conventional publicists have done for its domestic architecture so largely created by *nouveau-riche* cotton barons immediately before the Civil War. Still, however much the patriotism of these critics may have led them to exaggerate, there is something in the argument that a society like the South's—almost preindustrial in its economic and social organization and in its conception of life—has given the twentieth-century writers who grew up there certain advantages. They have known a world bound by the kind of traditions that give men a sense of the continuity of human experience, a world that has had a special cohesiveness and a powerful resistance to outside influences because of its defeat in the Civil War and yet has been kept from complacency by the agonizing moral dilemma posed for it by the Negroes in its midst, a problem that can be neither solved nor escaped.

Faulkner lived almost his whole life in Oxford, the county seat of Lafayette County, in Mississippi. By the time he was a grown man, it was evident enough that the old South was economically and even culturally in decline, but the natural effect of such decadence on a conservative people like Southerners is to make them cling to the old values and to dwell in a romantically exaggerated vision of the horror and the glory of life lived by these values, whether in the great days of the past or the desperate days of the present. Faulkner thus belonged to a culture with a tradition running from the pioneering struggles of the eighteenth and early-nineteenth centuries through a period of confident glory and heroic defeat in the mid-nineteenth century to a time of stubborn romantic refusal to recognize its twentieth-century decline, its final defeat by the shrewd and unscrupulous men of no family. Faulkner cannot keep from giving even these country-store businessmen with their carpetbagger souls a certain warped sense of glory, an inclination toward the gratuitous act, but in his novels about the Snopes family he shows clearly how they have destroyed the old families and their society, not so much because they are abler than because the old families care more for their honor than for their survival.

L

The bulk of Faulkner's work is devoted to his magnificent, brooding vision of the history of this culture. With his characteristic Southern passion for genealogy he has organized his image of it around a few families who live in Yoknapatawpha County—his fictional name for Lafayette County, Mississippi—and its county seat, which he calls Jefferson. There is the Sartoris family, whose history we know something about from the days of Colonel John Sartoris, who commanded a regiment in the Civil War, to the days when a pair of Sartoris twins were gallant, daredevil flyers in the first world war. There are the Snopeses, who emerge from the anonymity of the back country comparatively late in the story but end up owning most of Jefferson. There are the McCaslins, Faulkner's house of Atreus.

The McCaslins' history begins with Lucius Quintus Carothers McCaslin, who built a great plantation in Yoknapatawpha County early in the nineteenth century. He had two sons and a daughter by his white wife and a son by the mulatto daughter his first Negro mistress bore him. Just as he refused to recognize that this second Negro mistress was his own daughter, so he refused to recognize that her child was his son. He took ruthlessly whatever his all-too-human nature demanded, but he was too fiercely proud to admit he had such a nature or to betray himself by recognizing the existence of the human beings it led him to make his mistresses and his children.

Carothers' twin white sons devote their lives to trying to redeem his sin of inhumanity against the Negroes; they refuse to live in the great, unfinished plantation house their father had been building with slave labor: they themselves occupy a slave cabin and have their Negroes live in the plantation house. The heir of these twins, Isaac McCaslin—Carothers' only white heir in the male line of descent and the hero of Faulkner's greatest short story, "The Bear"—cannot endure even to own the plantation. He gives it to a cousin named Edmonds, who is descended from Carothers through his daughter, and goes to live in Jefferson, where he supports himself as a carpenter.

In 1938, an old man in his seventies, Ike goes on his annual hunting trip in the last remnant of virgin forest in Mississippi; it has been shrinking rapidly throughout his life. There, as he is lying in his tent early the first morning in camp, a girl comes in with a child in her arms and says to him, "You're Uncle Isaac." Since practically everyone in the county calls him that, it never occurs to him to think the girl means anything special by it; but presently something she says shows him she has Negro blood, and she says quietly, "Yes . . . I said you were Uncle Isaac." For she is not only part Negro; she is, like Ike, a descendant of Carothers McCaslin. Ike then discovers that the child in her arms is her son ("It's a boy, I reckon," Ike says to her with grim humor. "They usually are") by one of the men he has come on this hunting trip with, a man named Roth Edmonds who is also Ike's cousin, a descendant of Carothers McCaslin in the white line established by Carothers' daughter. After living some time with this girl, Roth Edmonds has discovered she has Negro blood and has deserted her. She has come looking for him now, not with any real hope, but because she cannot help herself. Understanding all this and filled with grief by it, Ike despairingly urges her to move North and to marry a man of her own race. She looks at him for a moment and then says quietly, "Old man, have you lived so long and forgotten so much that you don't remember anything you ever knew or felt or even heard about love?"

But Ike has not forgotten; it is only that he cannot escape what the history of four generations of McCaslin he knows so well makes him see, what the girl clearly knows in her heart too, that there is absolutely no hope for her. After nearly a hundred years of effort by Carothers McCaslin's descendants to redeem his sin of inhumanity against the Negroes, his rightful heir—the man who may repudiate his material inheritance from Carothers but cannot repudiate his inherited moral burden—must face the fact that the white descendant who bears Carothers' name has repeated Carothers' sin against the Negroes, compounding it, if not literally with incest, at least by committing it with a girl who is also a descendant of Carothers. How in these circumstances can he hope that the McCaslins—black or white —will ever be released from this crime? How can he give this girl any advice but the advice he does, even knowing very well before she tells him so that the humanity in her that Carothers McCaslin had begun by refusing to recognize in her great-great-great-grandmother still makes the advice futile? They are all doomed by the white McCaslins' refusal to recognize the humanity of the Negroes, even when they love them.

The sin of the McCaslin family is Faulkner's image of the sin committed—sometimes with arrogance, sometimes in agony—by a whole society. It is a sin of pride, a refusal to accept for itself the human condition. Often enough that pride makes for the kind of inhuman horror that resulted from Carothers McCaslin's unyielding arrogance, or that the stubborn heroism of Colonel Sartoris leads to when he has lived with it too long and done too much to satisfy it—"that transparent film [over the eyes] which the eyes of carnivorous animals have and from behind which they look at a world which no ruminant ever sees, perhaps dares to see, which I have seen before on the eyes of men who have killed too much, who have killed so much that never again so long as they live will they ever be alone." ("An Odor of Verbena")

But sometimes too this kind of pride makes for the comic arrogance of such characters as Lucas Beauchamp of *Intruder in the Dust*. Lucas Beauchamp is a Negro descendant of Carothers McCaslin—both his grandson and his great-grandson—and he possesses a gold toothpick and an ancient McCaslin hat as heirlooms to prove it: his full name is Lucas Quintus Carothers Beauchamp. He is mistakenly accused of murdering a white man and is saved from being lynched only by the heroic efforts of an indomitable elderly Southern gentlewoman, a small boy, and an eccentric intellectual lawyer. But when they save him from lynching and even prove him innocent, he does his best to repudiate the help they have given him. Like the McCaslin he is, he refuses to be obligated to anyone, even at the risk of his life.

When he is finally released from jail, the lawyer and the boy who have helped him are watching from the window of the lawyer's office. They see him "crossing the Square, probably at the same time [seeing]

the cocked hat and the thin fierce glint of the tilted gold toothpick."
Lucas comes straight to the lawyer's office to pay him, and the lawyer
finally agrees to accept two dollars—the cost of the fountain pen he
broke in exasperation when he was trying to make sense out of what
Lucas had been willing to tell him, in order to construct a defense.
Lucas counts out the two dollars in nickels and dimes and pennies and
then stands looking at the lawyer, who says, "Now what? What are
you waiting for now?" And Lucas says, "My receipt."

Lucas's refusal to admit he needs his fellow men is as fiercely arrogant as Carothers McCaslin's; but when that refusal is made—and
made with courage and cunning—by one of the downtrodden Negroes, against the white men who habitually monopolize arrogance,
then the shoe is suddenly on the other foot in a wonderfully comic
way. That Lucas owes his pride to his white ancestor, Carothers Mc-
Caslin, and even goes out of his way in good McCaslin style to display
his superiority to what he thinks of as the common white trash of the
community, is a further comic reminder of how hopelessly irrational
pride's refusal to accept its common humanity is.

Most strikingly of all, this pride is the source of heroism in Faulkner's work. His hero is characteristically a man who denies for the
sake of his pride the very obligation of living itself, as does the hero
produced by Faulkner's last important family, the Compsons. The
story of this hero is told in *The Sound and the Fury* (1929), a book
that also tells the story of Jason Compson, Faulkner's finest portrait
of a poor white, even though his name is Compson; he is, in fact,
precisely what the career of his legendary namesake suggests he is.
And it has Dilsey, who was modeled with loving care on the Negro
Mammy who brought up Faulkner himself and to whom he dedicated
The Sound and the Fury; she is undoubtedly the most magnificent
of all Faulkner's many portraits of Negroes, and she is something
greater than a hero. When Faulkner wrote a set of biographical notes
on the characters in *The Sound and the Fury* to help readers understand the genealogy of the Compsons, he headed one section of those
notes: "These others were not Compsons. They were black," and the

last name in this list is Dilsey's; of her Faulkner wrote simply, "They endured."

Four generations of Compsons appear in the novel, the oldest—Grandpa and Damuddy—only very briefly. The next generation consists of Jason Compson senior, his wife, Caroline Bascom Compson, and her ne'er-do-well brother, Maury Bascom. The Compsons have four children, Quentin, Candace, known in the family as Caddy, Jason, and Maury, who, when he is five, is discovered to be an idiot and is renamed Benjamin. Finally there is Caddy's illegitimate daughter whom she names Quentin for her beloved brother who is dead when Caddy's child is born. The Negroes consist of Dilsey, her husband, Roskus, their children, Versh, T. P., and Frony, and a grandchild named Luster.

The form of *The Sound and the Fury* is a daring experiment in the use of interior monologue; one of its main purposes is to give dramatic intensity to the narrative of a family tragedy that covers some forty years and has remoter echoes back as far as 1699. By imposing on his story the radical limitation of time required by interior monologue Faulkner reduces the present time of the novel to four days. These are, in the order in which they are presented in the novel: April 7, 1928, the day before Easter and also the thirty-third birthday of Benjy, the Compson's idiot youngest son, whose monologue covers the events of the day; June 2, 1910, which is covered by the monologue of Quentin Compson, then a student at Harvard, and is the day he commits suicide; April 6, 1928, which is covered in Jason Compson's monologue and describes his share in the family tragedy; and April 8, 1928, Easter Sunday, which is covered in the final section of the book and is the only one written in the third person; it is focused mainly on Dilsey.

Apart from these four days of the novel's present time, which the characters of course cover in detail in their monologues, their memories tend to cluster around a few dramatic occasions in the family's past history—the night Damuddy died in 1910, the few days of Caddy's disastrous love affair with Dalton Ames that left her two months pregnant when she hastily married Herbert Head in the spring of 1910; the day of that wedding, which is confused in the mind of Benjy—from whom we hear most about it—with the night of Damuddy's death (both involved large and unusual gatherings at the Compson house).

But we only gradually reconstruct for ourselves the Compson family's history, because it is presented to us only as it recurs in fragments in the memories of the characters whose interior monologues we overhear. Not only does this method of narration disrupt the order of events radically; it also presents these disordered events to us without explanation because the people who are remembering them know them too well to need to explain them to themselves; in the case of Benjy this lack of explanation goes even further, for well as he knows what he is remembering, Benjy does not understand most of it. What Faulkner gains by using this method is an uninterrupted view of his characters' innermost thoughts and feelings. In a conventional realistic novel the events of an action are presented in a temporal order; how a character knows these events, the order of the thoughts and feelings and memories which constitute his consciousness, can only be occasionally hinted at and must be largely reconstructed from such hints by the reader. In *The Sound and the Fury*—except for the last section, which is written in the third person—the consciousnesses of the characters are presented in the order that the ebb and flow of thoughts, feelings, and memories determine; the events of the action can only be hinted at when the thoughts and memories of the characters touch on them in some psychologically plausible way, and their temporal order must be largely reconstructed from such hints by the reader. What Faulkner has done, then, is to subordinate the historical reality of the temporal order of events to the psychological reality of the affective order of the consciousness.

This subordination is particularly marked in the monologue with which the novel begins, that of Benjy, the thirty-three-year-old idiot son. Though Faulkner presents his monologue in sentences, Benjy is dumb and does not think in words. His simple but powerful feelings—

his love of the Compson pasture, which is identified for him with the only happiness he has ever known, his love of his sister, Caddy, his love of firelight—these feelings govern the images that float through his mind and that are, as it were, translated into words for us by Faulkner. Benjy has no conscious conception of time, though he can suffer the losses it brings him; his mind moves freely from what is happening in the present to any incident in the past it reminds him of. His inability to conceive time is not merely a dramatic convenience for Faulkner; it is an important part of his theme.

What no Compson can endure is the outrage to his pride, the loss of dignity, imposed on him by his own time-bound nature. What Quentin will kill himself rather than endure is the temporal change that carries him and Caddy out of the timeless paradise of their childhood affection and brings Caddy to the fulfillment of her nature in her love for Dalton Ames and her pregnancy. Rather than admit that time can do that to him and Caddy, Quentin first insists that Caddy had no lover, that he and she have committed incest, and then—when Caddy does not join him in this grotesque and tragic fantasy but instead marries—he commits suicide. Throughout the day of his suicide, as if to emphasize his awareness that time is his real enemy, Quentin is obsessed by the ticking of the watch he has inherited from the past, from his grandfather. He tears off its hands and then listens sardonically to its incoherent ticking, "clicking away," as he says, "not knowing it couldn't even lie."

The reason Quentin so hates time is made clear in the conversation with his father—about his claim to have committed incest with Caddy—that he remembers just before he commits suicide.

. . . you wouldn't [he remembers his father saying] have been driven to the expedient of telling me you have committed incest [had you not been serious] and i i wasnt lying i wasnt lying and he you wanted to sublimate a piece of human folly into a horror and then exorcise it with truth and i it was to isolate her out of the loud noise of the world so that it would have to flee us of necessity and then the sound of it would be as though it had never been and he did you try to make her do it and i i was afraid she might and then it wouldnt have done any good but if i could tell you we did it would have been so and then the others wouldnt be so and then the world would roar away and he and now this other [Quentin's threat of suicide] you are not lying now either but you are still blind to what is in yourself to that part of general truth the sequence of natural events and their causes which shadows every man's brow even benjys you are not thinking of finitude you are contemplating an apotheosis in which a temporary state of the mind will become symmetrical above the flesh and aware both of itself and of the flesh it will not quite discard you will not even be dead.

Quentin then repeats over and over his father's word "temporary," "a temporary state of the mind." That is the horror for him, that he cannot command his own nature, that what he determines on in his mind cannot, by a transcendent act of his will, "become symmetrical above the flesh," but is at the mercy of time, is "temporary." His father understands him perfectly because at bottom he feels exactly the same way about time. "was," he says, "the saddest word of all there is nothing else in the world its not despair until time its not even time until it was." (Faulkner is writing in this unpunctuated style because all this is taking place in Quentin's memory, but it may help to punctuate a difficult passage like this, which then goes, " 'Was,' the saddest word of all. There is nothing else in the world. It's not despair until time [exists]; it's not even time until 'it was.' ")

Quentin may seem next to mad in his refusal to accept the reality of what his father calls "finitude," "the sequence of natural events and their causes that is in ourselves." But Quentin sees quite clearly that it is the flow of this temporal sequence of natural events that erodes every state of thought and feeling, however passionately it is determined on; it makes all states of the mind temporary, mere alms for oblivion. Quentin's father knows this too; he is as aware as Quentin that all the sound and fury, all the eloquent thought and heroic action of man's history, signify nothing. Quentin's father has accepted that as the truth, though he finds he cannot live with this truth and quietly drinks himself to death. Quentin defies it; he would rather die at once than suffer the humiliation time is sure to put upon him. As his father says to him with understanding and sympathy, "you cannot bear to think that someday it will no longer hurt like this now."

Only for Benjy, the idiot son with the defective sense of time, is there some escape from knowing what time does to men's commitments of feeling, though as Mr. Compson says to Quentin, it shadows even his brow. He too lost Caddy when she was married in 1910 and his beloved pasture was sold to a golf club to pay for the wedding and for Quentin's year at Harvard, and it is still a grief to him. Now, in 1928, he still goes every day to hang over the fence and look at the old pasture, and every time he hears a golfer say, "caddie," he howls with grief. Nevertheless, unlike Quentin and his father, he can live with Caddy in memory almost as if the past were present—though not quite: he always remembers Caddy in the past tense.

The novel opens with Benjy's interior monologue, on the morning of April 7, 1928, Benjy's birthday, and he has as usual gone to look at the pasture under the care of Luster, Dilsey's grandchild.

Luster came away from the flower tree and we went along the fence and they [the golfers] stopped and we stopped and I looked through the fence. . . .

"Here, caddie." He hit. They went across the pasture. I held to fence and watched them going away.

"Listen at you, now." Luster said. "Aint you something, thirty-three years old, going on that way. After I done went all the way to town to buy you that cake [which Dilsey has bought for Benjy's birthday]. Hush up that moaning. . . .

We went along the fence and came to the garden fence, where our shadows were. My shadow was higher than Luster's on the fence. We came to the broken place and went through it.

"Wait a minute." Luster said. "You snagged on that nail again. Cant you never crawl through here without snagging that nail."

With its defective sense of time, Benjy's mind then moves without transition to an occasion nearly thirty years earlier when he had been snagged on that same nail and Caddy had been with him.

> Caddy uncaught me and we crawled through. Uncle Maury said to not let anybody see us, so we better stoop over, Caddy said. Stoop over, Benjy. Like this, see. We stooped over and crossed the garden. . . .
> Keep your hands in your pockets, Caddy said. Or they'll get froze. You don't want your hands froze on Christmas, do you.

This memory of Caddy worrying over his cold hands makes Benjy's mind jump again to a time some ten years later than that Christmas.

> "It's cold out there." Versh said. "You don't want to go out doors." . . .
> "Let him go." Uncle Maury said. . . .
> We went out doors. The sun was cold and bright.
> "Where you heading for." Versh said. "You don't think you going to town, does you." We went through the rattling leaves. The gate was cold. "You better keep them hands in your pockets." Versh said. "You get them froze onto that gate, then what you do. Whyn't you wait for them in the house." He put my hands into my pockets. . . .
> Caddy was walking. Then she was running, her book satchel swinging and jouncing behind her.
> "Hello, Benjy." Caddy said. She opened the gate and came in and stooped down. Caddy smelled like leaves. "Did you come to meet me." She said. "Did you come to meet Caddy. What did you let him get his hands so cold for, Versh."

Then Benjy's mind is brought back to the present by Luster.

> What are you moaning about, Luster said. You can watch them again when we get to the branch. Here. Here's you a jimson weed. He gave me the flower.

In this way we are gradually made familiar with Benjy's mind and begin to recognize the extent to which his consciousness is governed by a few simple feelings, above all by his love of Caddy. He is aware only of what, in the most literal sense, happens. He experiences his love for Caddy, but he does not know it, has not sufficient powers of generalization to say to himself, "This is love." Nor does he know that it motivates his action, because his mind is incapable of thinking, "It is now time for Caddy to come home from school; I love her and want to go to the gate to meet her." He does not even know that thinking of Caddy makes him moan aloud; we learn this from what is to him the meaningless conversation of others.

In an important sense, this is the best possible kind of consciousness for Faulkner's purpose. Aware of events only as manifestations of its feelings about them—of what for Faulkner gives them their real meaning and value—and almost completely unconscious of their existence in time, it experiences what it lives by—its love—with a purity unknown to minds confused by the uncontrollable habit of looking before and after; and, since it knows almost no difference between "this now" and then, its feelings are unmodified by time. Their father is right when he tells Quentin that for him, "someday it will no longer hurt like this now." But for Benjy "this now" continues to exist forever almost as intensely as it did the moment it occurred. "Its not despair until time and its not even time until it was"; and as nearly as is possible it is never "it was" for Benjy.

These are the reasons Faulkner begins *The Sound and the Fury* with Benjy's interior monologue. For what is to him the significant aspect of reality, it is the most meaningful way (if, unfortunately, the most difficult one for readers to follow) of apprehending the experience the novel presents. It prepares us to understand Quentin's interior monologue which follows and which is, in content if not in appearance, more difficult than Benjy's because Quentin too can live only in the reality that Benjy lives in but knows, and therefore must fight his metaphysically complicated fight against, what Benjy is luckily barely conscious of, the meaningless temporal reality of his existence. As a consequence, Quentin's long monologue (it is almost half again as long as Benjy's), though much easier to follow in a superficial way, is more difficult to understand than Benjy's.

Quentin's monologue is followed by Jason's monologue of April 6, 1928, the day before the one covered by Benjy's opening monologue. Jason is, in his grim way, hilariously funny. He has all the egocentricity and the paranoid self-pity of his mother's side of the family combined with the stubborn pride and determination to stick to what they think right of the Compsons. His meanness and lack of scruple are equaled only by his assurance of his own rectitude and his almost heroic stoicism in the face of the universal conspiracy to make him suffer which he discovers all around him. He sees this conspiracy as impersonal, in the nature of things, and that gives him a kind of philosophic patience with it. Since Jason's feeling that things have been specially arranged to make him miserable is only an exaggerated version of what everyone feels at some time, we have a kind of reluctant sympathy with him as we watch him enduring his fate.

> I went out back to back the car out, then I had to go all the way round to the front [of the house] before I found them [the Negro servants].
> "I thought I told you to put that tire on the back of the car," I says.
> "I aint had time," Luster says. "Aint nobody to watch him [Benjy] till mammy git done in the kitchen."
> "Yes," I says, "I feed a whole damn kitchen full of niggers to follow around after him, but if I want an automobile tire changed, I have to do it myself."

By the spring of 1928, the time of Jason's monologue, both Quentin and his father are dead; Caddy has been divorced by Herbert Head when he discovered that her daughter—whom she names Quentin—is not his, and she has sent Quentin home to Jefferson to be brought up by Dilsey and has disappeared. She sends money regularly for Quentin, but Jason steals it and adds it to the hoard he is accumulating penny by penny from his salary as a clerk in the hardware store. He ought to have more than he does, but he has spent on an automobile the thousand dollars his mother gave him to buy a partnership in the hardware store. This automobile had become an absolute necessity to him when Herbert Head had given Caddy a car as an engagement present. It was an obvious part of the typical injustice of things that his sister, a mere woman, should have a car when he did not, and he had made up his mind on the spot to put this injustice right at the first opportunity. The first opportunity was when he had a chance to rob his mother and he had seized it with unhesitating courage.

It has made his life a good deal more difficult. He has to go through a complicated routine each month to keep his mother in ignorance, and his capital position has of course been weakened. Nonetheless, by 1928, his savings amount to $2,840.50, and with the money he has stolen from Quentin added to them, his capital comes to just short of $7,000. He keeps this money locked in his room because he is quite sure bankers are as crooked as the cotton brokers in New York who somehow manage to cheat him out of his money every time he takes a little fling on the cotton market ("Well, I reckon those eastern jews have got to live too. But I'll be damned if it hasn't come to a pretty pass when any damn foreigner that cant make a living in the country where God put him, can come to this one and take money right out of an American's pockets").

Living as he does entirely in the world as he knows it in his own consciousness, Jason is honestly unaware of the feelings of others; whatever they say or do he knows only as a part of the maddeningly unjust conspiracy to make it harder for Jason to have what he wants. He finds Quentin a special trial ("Once a bitch always a bitch, what I say"), and in his efforts to keep her in her place he overreaches himself, despite his cleverness. He makes her so miserable that in sheer desperation she climbs out of her bedroom window and around the outside of the house to the window of Jason's locked bedroom, breaks in, and steals his money. She then runs off with a man from a carnival and disappears forever. Jason's defeat is complete; he cannot even appeal effectively to the law, since he has himself stolen from Quentin better than half the money she has now stolen from him.

In his biographical notes on the Compsons, Faulkner describes

Jason as "the first sane Compson since before Culloden. . . . Logical rational contained and even a philosopher in the old stoic tradition: thinking nothing of God one way or the other . . . who was using his infant niece's illegitimacy to blackmail its mother." His self-pity convinces him of the special malice of everyone he has anything to do with and makes him sure that any piece of mean cleverness his ingenious mind conceives, however unscrupulous it may be, is simply a justified defense of his rights. As a result, he is completely defeated by a seventeen-year-old girl who is not malicious at all, only driven to desperate, self-destructive rebellion by the cruelty with which Jason —never in his self-righteousness suspecting what she feels—treats her.

Faulkner's statement in his biographical note on Jason that Jason "thinks nothing of God one way or the other" is not accidental; in a quiet way quite unlike the melodramatic religiosity of much twentieth-century literature, *The Sound and the Fury* is a religious book. In it the sound and fury of temporal existence—whether it be Caddy's passion or Quentin's defiance or Mr. Compson's despair—signify, for all their heroism and pathos, nothing. The only significant lives in *The Sound and the Fury* are Benjy's and Dilsey's, and only Dilsey grasps their significance.

In the book's last section we watch Dilsey doing what she has been doing all her life, that is, keeping the Compson family in existence. It is as humble and homely a job as can be imagined. Dilsey cooks and washes, keeps Mrs. Compson as happy as her inexhaustible self-pity will allow her to be, brings up two generations of Compson children, and takes care of the idiot Benjy. It is all done with an unobtrusive love whose source we discover when Dilsey goes off to the services— it is Easter Day—at her Negro church, taking with her Benjy, who, Faulkner reminds us again, is exactly the age Jesus was when he was crucified. At the climax of the service, the eloquent, monkey-faced Negro minister slides from the correct, white man's English in which he had begun his sermon into the Negroes' own language and cries: "O breddern! I sees de doom crack en hears de golden horns shoutin down de glory, en de arisen dead whut got de blood en de ricklickshun

of de Lamb!" And "in the midst of the voices and the hands, Ben
sat, rapt in his sweet blue gaze. Dilsey sat bolt upright beside him,
crying rigidly and quietly in the annealment and the blood of the remembered Lamb."

They are Faulkner's pure in heart, the one by inescapable innocence of the world, the other by the triumph of her faith and love
over her knowledge of the world. For no one has understood better
than Dilsey the tragedy of the Compsons. She has cared for them
with unfaltering devotion, however little they may have deserved it,
however hopeless she saw her efforts to be. Now she has seen the
last of them—the seventeen-year-old Quentin—irretrievably lost, as
she had seen Quentin's mother, Caddy, and her uncle Quentin and
her grandfather lost before her. Only, unlike the rest of them, Dilsey
has seen this family history in the light of the faith she has just so
movingly renewed. Characteristically Faulkner reminds us, at the very
moment he is showing us Dilsey's vision of what this history truly
means, that like all the others Dilsey lives in time. He does so by sur-
rounding this moment with the incongruous human comedy of Negro
social life. Dilsey treats most of her acquaintances with a comic social
scorn that expresses quite literally Faulkner's judgment of all men.
"What [we] need," Dilsey says, "is a man kin put de fear of God into
dese here trifling young niggers." When they address her, however
respectfully—"Sis' Gibson! How you dis mawnin?"—she will not
answer them unless they are quite old; her daughter Frony has to keep
up the amenities—"Mammy aint feeling well dis mawnin."

When Dilsey is walking back from church, back into the unavoidable world of time that no Compson except Benjy has ever been able
to endure, she continues to cry. It offends Frony's sense of the social
decencies.

"Whyn't you quit dat, mammy? Wid all dese people looking.
We be passing white folks soon."

"I've seed de first en de last," Dilsey said. "Never you mind
me."

"First en last what?" Frony said.

"Never you mind," Dilsey said. "I seed de beginning, en now I sees de endin."

What Dilsey has seen is not merely the temporal, historical reality of the Compsons, whom she has known from the first to the last member of the family, but also the paradoxical reality of that history's timeless meaning. Dilsey is remembering—and believing—the promise of "I am Alpha and Omega, the beginning and the end, the first and the last."

M

JAMES GOULD COZZENS
1903-

Guard of Honor
1948

James Gould Cozzens is half a generation younger than Dos Passos,
Fitzgerald, and Faulkner, and his background differs from theirs in a
way that would not have concerned Dos Passos and Faulkner but
would have aroused Fitzgerald's envy. Cozzens' background is conservative upper-middle class, almost exactly what Fitzgerald always
wished his had been. "I spent my youth," Fitzgerald once said, "in
alternately crawling in front of the kitchen maids and insulting the
great" because it was not. He could never stop thinking of himself as
a *parvenu;* Cozzens has the assurance, even arrogance, of a man who
has never known a moment's doubt that he is not. He also has the
admirably tough-minded rationalism of his kind, and the outspoken
honesty of his treatment of sex in *By Love Possessed* offended a good
many readers—including some pretty advanced thinkers—who pride
themselves on their liberalism and are eager to defend equally detailed
accounts of sexual acts when they are glamorized by transcendental
rhetoric of one kind or another.

Cozzens comes of a family that lived for over a century in Newport,
Rhode Island, where his great-grandfather was mayor of the town
and governor of the state during the Civil War. Cozzens himself grew

up on Staten Island, then a rural suburb of New York, and was educated at Kent and Harvard. He was precociously intelligent and once drove Kent's famous headmaster, Dr. Sill, into a formidable rage by arguing with him about religion. ("I was the boy intellectual who didn't believe in God, scorned healthy exercise, and subscribed to *The New Republic*.")

At Harvard he was something of a dandy, a friend of Lucius Beebe, and even a gay dog. In the middle of his second year there he had his first novel published and left to write—temporarily, as he then supposed, but in fact for good. After several years of wandering—in Canada and Cuba and Europe—he married a talented literary agent named Bernice Baumgarten. It is characteristic of Cozzens' blunt toughness of mind that he should have said of this marriage, "Mother almost died when I married a Jew, but later when she saw I was being decently cared for, she realized that it was the best thing that could have happened to me." During the war Cozzens served for three years in the Army Air Force, where he rose to the rank of major. Otherwise he and his wife have lived in comfortable and almost complete seclusion. "My social preference," he has said, "is to be left alone, and people have always seemed willing, even eager to gratify my inclination."

Because of this inclination Cozzens has never participated in the literary politics and public-relations activities to which most writers devote a good deal of their energy; in any event, his views would, as it amuses him to recognize, make him ineligible. "I am more or less illiberal," he says, "and strongly antipathetic to all political and artistic movements. I was brought up an Episcopalian and where I live the landed gentry are Republican." He thinks the whole bag of tricks about the alienation of the artist and intellectual in America is absurd and that, if anything, such people get more attention than they deserve. "I," he says with his own kind of irony about American advertising culture, "am considered a man of distinction because I write books. The truth is, we don't deserve it."

None of this should suggest that Cozzens lacks compassion or is

unaware of the defects of the world he lives in. In fact the amusement
at himself and the irony about the world in all these remarks suggest
precisely the opposite. But unlike most writers of his period, Cozzens
feels a strong obligation to see the world for what it is: not to be content with it, but to recognize its nature and its strength. "People get
a very raw deal from life," he says, ". . . [but] life is what life is." All
this makes him an almost subversive figure in an age when sentimental anarchism and "enlightened" political views have hardened into
an intellectual convention as tyrannical as bourgeois moralism is supposed once to have been, and when keeping in good standing in the
intellectual party is almost obligatory.

Cozzens has paid a price for his independence. For years he was
the most unpublicized writer of anything like his talent in America,
and when, with the publication of *By Love Possessed,* it looked for
a moment as if he might get the recognition he deserved, Dwight Mac-
Donald, the ablest critic of his kind in New York, made a carefully
planned attack on Cozzens that undoubtedly damaged his reputation.
From Mr. MacDonald's point of view, it was a wise move; Cozzens'
novels represent a conception of experience that is a danger to what
Mr. MacDonald cares about.

Like H. L. Mencken before him, Mr. MacDonald lives amidst the
continuous skirmishing of the endless war intellectuals of his kind
conduct against their society. It keeps them too occupied to notice
that, so far as literature is concerned, they are fighting yesterday's bat-
tles, rushing anxiously to the defense of a kind of novel that no doubt
did need—and seldom got—critical support a decade or two ago but
is almost too easily admired today. The conception of experience in
this kind of novel accords with the ideological position taken up by
people like Mr. MacDonald and they are therefore very busy rescuing
such novels from a neglect they no longer suffer. In this way their
criticism becomes largely political, maneuvers in the damaging war
of the clerks, whose object is an impossible unconditional surrender.
It does not make them love their victims any better that they refuse
to play this ideological game and will not even fire off a letter to the

press in their own defense. Cozzens tries them particularly high. He is, as Bernard De Voto said a long time ago, simply not "a literary man, he is a writer. There are a handful of them in every age. Later on it turns out they were the ones who wrote the age's literature."

Cozzens' respect for life as it is gives him an exceptional interest in the actual world. This interest ranges all the way from his pleasure in the ingenious organization of things like department stores and air force bases to his almost anthropological curiosity about the customary life of social institutions like the small town or of professions like the law and medicine. He has a deep respect for men who can function effectively in the world, whether they are skilled mechanics or talented pilots, able generals or smart judges, and this respect, because it is not dictated by a theory, is without condescension. Both *The Just and the Unjust* (1942) and *By Love Possessed* (1957) are legally impeccable novels about the law; the hero of *The Last Adam* (1933) is a doctor, and the hero of *Men and Brethren* (1936) is a priest. Three of these four novels show a fascinated intimacy with the social life of the American small town. *Guard of Honor* (1948) is a novel about life on an Army Air Force Base during the war; no one has ever been able to find a flaw in its minutely detailed account of that life.

Because of this respect for the actual world, Cozzens represents it with a fullness and a lack of distortion by self-interest very unusual in American literature. He is himself a man of very considerable intelligence; the actions of his novels are bathed in a glow of brilliant good sense that is a continuous pleasure, and the intellectual powers of his clever characters are actually demonstrated in his novels, not, as is so often the case in novels, merely asserted to exist. At the same time his respect for the actual world will not let him distort what it is in order to convince us that it can—or at least ought to—be what he would like it to be, though the temptation to do so must attack him as often as it does any intelligent man. He can see as quickly as anyone how raw the deal most people get from life is, but he never allows himself to forget that "life is what life is."

Cozzens confronts squarely the rawness of the deal that drives the subjective novelists to a defiance of life itself. He knows as well as Melville and Faulkner how strong the passions of the heart are. But since he never loses sight of the simple, obvious fact that life is what life is, he is always conscious that it is not what these passions so often convince men it is, or may be. To him their effect on men is a kind of possession—in the sense of being influenced to the point of madness.

By Love Possessed is a magnificently organized representation of every variety of amatory possession. There, side by side, in the most natural way imaginable, we see the most gross and primitive sorts of lust striking without consideration every kind of person, from the low-grade moron to the most self-possessed of men, and the most sub-tilized—and, if one will, neurotic—kinds of self-sacrificing affection. It throws a flood of light on the characteristic difference between Cozzens' sense of reality and that of novelists like Faulkner to see how Cozzens deals with the situation that drives Quentin Compson of *The Sound and the Fury* to suicide.

The hero of *By Love Possessed,* Arthur Winner, loses his wife by a miscarriage. Some years later, one of his friends, worrying over the danger to his own wife's life when she insists on getting pregnant in spite of having been told it is dangerous for her, says to Arthur Winner impatiently, "Well, you ought to know!" He is immediately filled with remorse; but Arthur Winner says to him, "I ought to know; and I do. I don't mind your saying it, Fred." Then Cozzens shows us Arthur Winner facing, with the stoicism that is typical of Cozzens' heroes, the fact of life that Quentin Compson flatly refused to face, the fact that Quentin's father made explicit when he said to Quentin of his feelings about Caddy's marriage, "You cannot bear to think that someday it will no longer hurt like this now." Arthur Winner is faced at this moment in *By Love Possessed* by that "someday"; and he finds Quentin's father was quite right.

In a way that Fred Dealey, intent on his immediate anxiety of looking forward, imagining what could come, not able to see things as a looking-back would see them, might be unable to understand, Arthur Winner spoke the truth [when he said, "I don't mind your saying it"]. The truth was one that took getting used to. Discovering it, the heart reluctant, had recourse to customary defenses, tried to add one more to the index of prohibited thoughts. This truth, the fact that the heart's dear feelings, conceived as spiritual, could also die; that the poor flesh, supposed to be ephemeral, outlasted them with ease, at first sight simply would not do. For a second sight; for an adjustment to the knowledge that this, being so, would simply have to do, a little more time was needed. Contrite, Fred Dealey swore when he thought of the pain he must have caused any man of decent feeling. Forgiven, he was crediting Arthur Winner with magnanimity, not with a plain statement of the case.

Here Arthur Winner faces the same truth that Quentin Compson and his father faced, that "the heart's dear feelings" are easily outlasted in time by the "poor flesh." But how different the response to that fact. For Quentin and his father, "the heart's dear feelings" were the only reality that mattered. Rather than allow them to die, rather than allow the reality of his consciousness—"this now"—to gradually change, he will destroy the poor flesh which makes "someday" able to work its will on him. His father sees the defect in this line of reasoning, the assumption that Quentin's consciousness will somehow survive death intact, preserved forever in "this now," that what he calls ironically a "temporary" state of the mind "will become symmetrical above the flesh and . . . you will not even be dead." Quentin's father sees that only religious faith of a kind neither he nor Quentin has will support such reasoning and that even such faith will not justify Quentin's assumption that he can make his merely human love of Caddy immortal. He sees that, but knows no better than Quentin an endurable alternative.

There is an endurable alternative for Arthur Winner. The truth that "the heart's dear feelings" are more ephemeral than the flesh, "being so, would simply have to do." It would have to do because "life is what life is." The only choice open to a man is to make do with it or to cease immediately—if possible (as it almost certainly will not be) upon the midnight with no pain. Moreover, he regards the final defense of the heart's dear feelings, the one that offers systematic justification for its "index of prohibited thoughts"—that is, religion—at best, "not as shedding light on, but as admitting, the mystery, awesome and permanent, of life." At worst, it seems to Arthur Winner an "assemblage of phrases that [have] no exact significance, of tautological terms, of proofless postulations" that a good many people, with quite remarkable arrogance, insist on men's accepting.

Here, then, is what the problem of time and mortality is for the man who finds outer reality the significant one and is convinced that freedom is the recognition of necessity, the recognition that life is what life is. An equally striking consequence of Cozzens' commitment to this aspect of reality is that his novels are written in a form a good many readers have almost forgotten about. Their subtlety is of an old-fashioned kind that often baffles critics accustomed to the "modern" novel. Not for Cozzens the ingenious resources of the experimental novel for making the consciousness more real to the reader than events. There are no obvious symbols in his novels; no myths peer out at us from behind the stories; no claims are made in them that writers have some special, mystical knowledge that readers may not understand but should be appropriately awed by. Faced by this absence of the familiar, fashionable devices for giving novels a range and depth of subjective reality, critics are inclined to jump to the conclusion that Cozzens' novels have no subtlety. Unprepared for the different kind of subtlety the novelist of objective reality is concerned with, they simply miss the beautiful, intricate pattern that makes every one of the minutely observed realistic events in Cozzens' novels contribute to his meaning, to his vision of what life is, without the help of any distortion of objective reality or any special rhetorical appeal.

For a writer like this, one of the most attractive qualities in men is their ability to take pleasure in what life offers them, their natural responsiveness to the drama that is always a part of the ordinary business of life. His novels are full of attractively unintellectual—though often quite impressively talented—men of action (a very rare kind of character in modern fiction) who take an amusingly unliterary delight in such things ("Say, is that a nice sight! Pretty as a picture, you ask me! Say, I'm glad I saw this! Makes you think, Nat"). Cozzens particularly sympathizes with such responsiveness when it occurs in unpretentious people. For him the natural point of view for observing the arrival of a couple of generals at an air base, for instance, is that of the girls in the control tower. From there he can contemplate with satisfaction the ingenious arrangements of the tower itself and the handling of the generals' plane; he can watch with a pleasure whose simplicity amuses him the earnestly executed, unsophisticated military ceremony for receiving generals; above all he can share the happy enthusiasm—not without its quite unawed critical alertness—with which the girls in the tower enjoy the spectacle.

"Oh, I want to see this," T/5 Bell said. "Can I see them get out?"

"All right," [said T/3 Anderson.] "And you can too, Keller. Only, bring your microphone. It'll reach. So if anyone calls—"

Shoulder to shoulder they pressed against the convex glass panel.

Under them, the C-60 wheeled and swung broadside. There was a pause while the engines were run up. Then the cabin door opened. A faint harsh voice rose, bawling: "Present—arms!" The big black drum major let his lifted baton fall; the eight snare drums, beaten, jumped to a fine muted racket of ruffles; the eight lifted trumpets blew out a high blaring flourish.

"My, he's cute!" said T/3 Anderson. "General Nichols! Unless this is the other one. He looks like, you know in the movies, that tall, quiet man—"

T/5 Murphy said, clasping her hands, "Oh, let me see, Mona! Just for a minute—"

T/3 Anderson handed over the glasses.

"That other one, I don't think he's so hot! General Baxter! Who is he, anyway?"

"Search me! They have hundreds of generals—"

"Oh, can I see now! Please, Rose—"

For the same reason Cozzens lingers over such moments as the one that occurs after seven paratroopers have been accidentally drowned. Like an historical painter fully aware of all the things that are supposed to be wrong with historical paintings who also knows that the response they evoke can be genuinely common and not merely commonplace, he treats such moments with loving care.

The hot sun, near the horizon, poured a dazzling gold light across the great reach of the air field. Under a pure and tender wide sky . . . the flat light bathed everything. . . . Around the two generals a circle of officers had gathered, posed in concern. In this sad, gold light their grouping made a composition like that found in old-fashioned narrative paintings of classical incidents or historical occasions—the Provost Marshall indicated the lake with a demonstrative gesture; a young Air Force captain faced him, standing tense and stiff. Bulky in his fighting trim, a captain of paratroopers, and Major McIlmoyle, helmeted and dirty, waited in sombre attitudes like legates who had brought news of a battle. To one side, a lieutenant colonel . . . in stylized haste gave grave tidings to a thin chicken colonel, that instant arrived. . . .

Near the end of *Guard of Honor* someone mentions providing a guard of honor for the dead, and young General Beal, the reasonable but impatient man of action, says to Colonel Ross, the middle-aged reserve officer—a judge in civilian life—who is his Air Inspector:

"I don't know what good a guard of honor does him when he's dead. . . . Some more goddamn ceremony! How about you, Judge?"

Colonel Ross, not without grandiloquence, said: "It does us good. Ceremony is for us. The guard, or as I think we now prefer to call it, escort of honor is a suitable mark of our regret for mortality and our respect for service—we hope, good; but if bad or indifferent, at least, long . . . . it ought to get a man something. . . . Something people can see."

Laughing, General Beal said: "That's telling them, Judge! Only, what I meant was: how about another drink?"

These quotations are from *Guard of Honor,* Cozzens' finest novel. The present time of *Guard of Honor* covers a little more than three days in the middle of 1943 at a large United States Army Air Force Base at Ocanara, Florida, the headquarters of AFORAD, the Army Airforces Operations and Requirements Analysis Division. Nothing melodramatic occurs during these three days; there are only the usual troubles and confusions—the near-crash of General Beal's plane during a landing, the tension caused by the arrival of a group of Negro flyers at the base, the accidental deaths of seven paratroopers during a practice jump. But Cozzens fits into these three days, either as direct or as recollected action, a large variety of scenes that cover every aspect of the base's life and an astonishing number of fully developed characters—there are over fifty of them. Though the novel's many scenes deliberately carry us from one end of the base to the other, the tight chronological arrangement allows Cozzens to follow closely three major actions—and a dozen minor ones—each focused on a central character from whose point of view we follow the events he is involved in.

The second day of the novel's present time, for example, begins with one of Cozzens' characteristic descriptions of a time-honored ceremony, the sounding of reveille, a ceremony that now comes to a climax in an appealingly unintentional irony when the Sergeant of the Guard, at precisely 6:25 A.M., drops the needle on a scratchy record and the notes of reveille crash rousingly out of a hundred loudspeakers throughout the base. We are then taken in turn to the awakening of a series of characters, each of whom is at the center of one of the novel's actions. First we see Lieutenant Amanda Turck awakening from a troubled sleep in the WAAC barracks and struggling to arouse her friend Mary Lippa from her wholly untroubled rest. Then "two miles away to the west, in the hospital area, [we see] . . . Lieutenant Werthauer, the Night Duty Officer, . . . yawning and listening for the [Morning] Gun." We hear that gun at the Oleander Towers, a decayed resort hotel in the town of Ocanara where the more fortunate of the base's officers live. There its faint sound catches Colonel Ross, the Air Inspector, entering the hotel dining room and confronting over breakfast the day's first nagging problem, the local newspaper's daily sniping at base policy. The distant but still distinct boom of the Morning Gun also awakens Captain Nathaniel Hicks in his bedroom in the hotel suite he shares with two other officers.

In civilian life Captain Hicks is the editor of a large magazine and he has therefore been assigned to one of the base's innumerable special projects, a manual on Pursuit Aviation.

He understood well enough that he belonged to that undistinguished majority of men for whom it should no doubt be a mortification that work was an end in itself, not a necessary detested means to make a living, certainly not a shrewd enterprise whose motive and hope was some blissful future state of living without work. His bliss was here and now; there was no pastime like the press of business. . . . To abhor this fantastic existence, to miss his wife and home, to regret the work, so much more important and interesting, that the war had interrupted, Nathaniel Hicks would have to wait for the proper moment, the unforeseen lull in the bustle, the speaking trifle's abrupt impression on the mind, to tell him the truth that there was a war on, and that he, amazingly, was in it.

With this passage we come to the controlling feeling about life in *Guard of Honor,* the feeling of that undistinguished majority of men whose pleasure in the press of business is regularly interrupted by the speaking trifle's abrupt impression. Only the night before Nathaniel Hicks had lain sleepless in the BOQ at a neighboring base considering his day's work, a consultation with a fighter pilot named Post, who has lost an arm in combat. Unreconciled to his loss, Major Post has disagreed rudely with what all the other experts have told Captain Hicks about Pursuit Aviation.

Considering the conflicts in the material, Nathaniel Hicks' editorial training told him what should be done. You just shelved it. . . . Two years ago, decisions like this were left to him; . . . they were not left to him here. . . . Never mind! Prepare [the manual] anyway! Arrange these papers alphabetically and burn them! . . .

War reversed accustomed order and upset reasoned expectation. Constantly halted, blankly amazed, a man must ask himself what in God's name he was doing here. . . . The accessible and obvious explanations of how you came to be where you were involved only motives and choices of your own. They hardly seemed good enough to settle the disquieted mind's question, or still the primary amazement which recognized that it was preposterous. Major Post must find it preposterous to have no left arm. Major Post always had two arms, in very much the sense that Nathaniel Hicks always, or at least since he left college, had a rational life. . . . He and Major Post regarded their present circumstances with dismay and incredulity—not exactly sorry for themselves; not necessarily complaining; but deeply and disturbingly aware that this they would not have chosen.

Here was nothing they had elected to do and did. This was done to them. The dark forces gathered, not by any means at random or reasonlessly, but according to a plan in the nature of things, like the forces of a storm; which, as long as heat expanded air and cold contracted it, would have to proceed. When the tempest reached its hurricane violence, uprooting, overturning, blowing away, you must make the best of its million freaks, whose diverse results might range from riddling Major Post's arm with a burst of 7.7 mm Japanese bullets to landing Nathaniel Hicks in his sweat-soaked underwear on a cot in the dark at Sellers Field.

The epigraph of *Guard of Honor* makes the same point; it is from Ariel's speech in *The Tempest* when he reminds the traitors that "the elements/ Of which your swords are temper'd may as well/ Wound the loud winds, or with bemock'd-at stabs/ Kill the still closing waters" as try to oppose these ministers of Fate. The operations of Fate are not incomprehensible, random and reasonless, as Nathaniel Hicks put it; but, like the forces of nature, they proceed inexorably. All a man can do is make the best of them, and make the best of them is what Cozzens' admirable characters do, just as his foolish characters, kicking hard against the pricks, make the worst of them. Always conscious of the real nature of things, the admirable characters devote their energies to trying to impose a meaningful pattern on the ordinary disorder of human affairs. They find their satisfaction in the press of business itself, but they are well aware, especially as they grow older, of the melancholy spectacle of their mortality. But "Downhearted," as Colonel Ross thinks at his moment of greatest trial, "[is] no man's part. A man must stand up and do the best he can with what there is. . . . If mind failed you, seeing no pattern; and heart failed you, seeing no point, the stout, stubborn will must be up and doing. A pattern should be found; a point should be imposed."

Cozzens' heroes are the men who are trying to be responsible for the continuity and order of life in a world of dangerously childish though often well-intentioned men, each of whom is "like a chess player who had in his head no more moves than the one it was now his turn to make. He would be dumbfounded when, after he had made four or five such moves (each sensible enough in itself), sudden catastrophe, from an unexpected direction by an unexpected means, fell on him, and he was mated."

The people in *Guard of Honor* are of two kinds that are best represented by the two central characters. General Beal, at forty the youngest major general in the United States Army, has been put in command of Ocanara to give him the administrative experience he will need to command the Tactical Air Force in the expected invasion of Japan. He is by nature a man of action and has already proved himself a fine flier and group commander. But he is a reasonable man of action who recognizes the need to deal with the situation he finds himself in, whatever it may be, and knows there are problems that flying, however skilful, will not solve. Colonel Ross, effectively though not officially General Beal's second in command, is a similarly reasonable man of thought, trained by a lifetime in the law to sort out and deal with the absurdly unreasonable but formidable impulses of ordinary men. The essential quality these two men have in common is demonstrated by Colonel Ross in a discussion with his wife of the problem created at Ocanara by the newly activated group of Negro officers.

A great many people, maybe most people, confronted by a definite situation, one in which they don't know what to do, get nowhere because they are so busy pointing out that the situation should be remade so they *will* know what to do. Whether you like it or not, there are things you can't buck—no matter how much you want to, how vital it is to you. A parachutist who jumps from an airplane cannot climb back, no matter what. . . . Gravity is a condition, not a theory. . . . For reasons of justice and decency; and also for reasons of political policy, the War Department decided that colored men must have a chance to qualify as officers . . . [and] an unmanageably large number of [the white officers on the Base] hold that a nigger is a nigger. They will not have anything to do with him socially. . . . I don't say this couldn't be changed, or that it won't ever be; but it won't change today, tomorrow, this week. A man cannot choose to see what he cannot see.

Beside each of these central characters stands a group of lesser ones, the degree of whose effectiveness is determined by the extent to which they control their impulse to remake the actual situation into one they can handle. In each of these groups there is one character of unusual abilities who indulges this impulse without restraint and serves as a contrast to his responsible counterpart. For General Beal this character is his copilot, Benny Carricker. Carricker is a talented pilot with an almost incredible combat record for whom everything except flying is "all this crap." When General Beal's plane is almost wrecked by another plane that—through no fault of its pilot—lands at the same time, Carricker saves the general and his party by an astonishing piece of flying. Then, when they have landed safely, he walks across the apron and slugs the pilot of the other plane.

He does not consider whose fault the near-accident really was, and the last thing he would notice or care about (being below rather than above racial prejudice) is that this pilot is a Negro. He thus precipitates the social crisis that only the combined efforts of General Beal and Colonel Ross finally resolve. Carricker's arrogant disregard of everything he has decided is crap is quite innocent. When what seems to him his obviously just attack on the Negro pilot makes terrible trouble, not least of all for him, he can only ascribe this surprising turn of events to the malice of a world he never made and thinks he can afford to want no part of.

The contrasting character to Colonel Ross is Lieutenant Edsell, a man as gifted intellectually as Carricker is in action. Edsell lives in a continuous state of heady irritation because the world fails to conform promptly to what he sincerely believes to be the commonsense social theories he has adopted. He is convinced that the immediate realization of a state of things everybody must see is right is being prevented only by the mulish stupidity of men who are undoubtedly less intelligent than he is. Since the actual situation that confronts him is never what his theory tells him it must be, since he always has things at least half wrong, he is always unsuccessful. Yet whenever he fails, he goes down to defeat, like Carricker, dignified by his very real and—within their limits—very useful talents and by the pathos of his inability to understand where he has gone wrong.

Confident that the whole problem of the Negro pilots is the consequence of the stupid illiberality of everyone in authority on the post, Edsell sets out happily to confound these authorities, to pin back the ears of every officer of field grade in sight. It is a kind of activity in which he takes real pleasure, for

> . . . practice in giving and taking injuries and insults had plainly taught Lieutenant Edsell to study anyone with whom he found himself often in altercation; and the insight he then demonstrated was disconcerting. He knew where to aim. . . . His hit made, Lieutenant Edsell, too delighted by his success to be very malevolent about it, savored your reaction. Whether you howled, or whether you ludicrously pretended that he never touched you, it was all one to him—equally satisfactory.

When he confidently asserts his inaccurate version of the affair of the Negro pilot ("[The unreconstructed Confederates] gathered in suitable force . . . and when a colored medium bomber crew came in and landed, they jumped them. . . ."), Amanda Turck, who had been there, says "I don't believe that ever happened. I—"

"No, you don't. That's right," Lieutenant Edsell said. "That's the reason a lot of sadistic sub-morons down in dear old Dixie can do whatever they want to any Negro, any time. When you're told about it, you don't believe it. . . . Well, just take my word for this. It did happen. A lot of things you don't know about happen every day in the South. And a lot of things you don't know about happen every day in the Army. But never worry your pretty heads! Just keep not knowing about them, and you'll be fine."

People like Carricker and Edsell are always ready to make the most of the muddles created by well-meaning people who never see beyond the next move and always make that by the book, regardless of circumstances. This is the process by which the storm blows up, a process that is perfectly explicable but largely uncontrollable. It is what produces the customary disorder of the world out of which the reasonable men of action and of thought must try to produce, if not order, at least an operable situation. By "busting a gut," as General Beal puts it, he and Colonel Ross finally manage to avert the worst consequences of the situation nearly everyone on the post has contributed something to and Carricker and Edsell have, in their innocent righteousness, done their best to make worse. By the end of the novel's third day, Ocanara's problems have been, if not solved, at least contained. Pausing to look back at them, General Beal says to Colonel Ross:

"Judge, I have some little weaknesses, like having to do things my own way; and Jo-Jo thinks I'm just a fly boy, and I am. No, I'm no master mind; but spell it out for me, and I'll pretty often get it. You tell me what you think I don't know, and I'll tell you what I think you don't know; and we'll get there." . . .

"I'll try," Colonel Ross said. "An old man like me, a man I knew once—he was a judge, too—used to say: *sed quis costodiet ipsos custodes*. Know what that means?"

"Hell, no," General Beal said. "There are quite a few things I don't know."

"Well, in this case it might mean, who's going to pick up after me."

N

General Beal slapped his shoulder lightly. "I could take care of that when it happens," he said. "I'll do the best I can, Judge; and you do the best you can; and who's going to do it better?"

Who indeed? Both these men have what General Beal is amused to call their "little weaknesses," of a kind inherent in their natures as men of action and of thought; it is almost the best part of their wisdom always to keep those limitations in mind, for they are both reasonable men. It is men like them who keep the world going, in spite of its natural tendency to fall back into inoperable disorder, in spite of the efforts of more talented and less reasonable men than they to make that disorder worse.

Because Cozzens respects and, indeed, loves the actual world even though he knows its evils and inadequacies as well as those who cannot endure it, and because he has the capacity—rare among intellectuals of any kind—to recognize how much unspectacular talent and effort it requires to keep that world in working order, he has written at a very high level a kind of novel that is unusual both in substance and in form in American fiction, particularly in the twentieth century. For anyone not blinded by the spectacular achievements of the great, impassioned idealists who have written many of the twentieth century's best novels, Cozzens' achievement must have a special interest, precisely because he does realize with astonishing insight and intelligence an aspect of our experience that has almost disappeared from serious fiction and that confronts us in his novels like a new discovery. In order to do so he has recreated the full-scale realistic novel—the kind that deals with the manners, not of a limited class and kind of people, but a whole society—for a culture that has scarcely ever seen itself before in that undistorting mirror. It is a remarkable achievement, and the reader who misses its meaning because of some mistaken belief that this kind of subject or this kind of form is somehow intrinsically inferior to the kinds that interest Melville or Faulkner is robbing himself as surely as the much rarer reader who does the opposite.

ROBERT PENN WARREN
1905-

All the King's Men
1946

Robert Penn Warren has had at least four careers as a writer. He has written six volumes of poems, one of which, *Promises,* won him the Pulitzer Prize in 1957; his *Selected Poems* won the Bollingen award for 1966. He had already received the Pulitzer Prize for Fiction in 1946 with *All the King's Men,* the third of his eight novels. He has written a biography of John Brown and two books on segregation. He has been one of the important contributors to the critical renaissance of the twentieth century and found (with Cleanth Brooks) a way to make its insights available to students in the most influential textbook of our time, *Understanding Poetry.* There is something symbolic about this last achievement, for the most persistent of Mr. Warren's beliefs is that men must, at whatever cost, carry knowledge into the world, must live their daily lives by its lights, and must subject it to the test of experience.

Mr. Warren is usually thought of as a member of the Fugitive Group that gathered in the 1920's at Vanderbilt, where the young Warren studied with John Crowe Ransom and roomed for a time with Allen Tate. It is difficult to imagine a better apprenticeship in the craft of writing than working with Ransom, and to have been exposed

to the grace, the wit, and the violence of Allen Tate's mind must have
been almost too stimulating. Yet the association of Warren with the
Fugitives is misleading, too. There were other important influences in
his life, at California and Yale and Oxford, where he did graduate
work, and wherever it was that he acquired the attitude—very different from either Ransom's or Tate's—that he has always had.

The starting point for that attitude—as for the different one taken
by Mr. Tate—is the problem of self-realization and self-possession.
The speaker in Mr. Tate's "Ode to the Confederate Dead" can

> praise the vision
> And praise the arrogant circumstance
> Of those who fall
> Rank upon rank, hurried beyond decision,

but they are not real to him; he cannot share their vision or even
truly understand it, though for a moment of pious respect for the past
he imagines them rising like demons out of the earth. What is real
for him is their tombstones, as neatly aligned as their ranks had been,
decaying slowly in a neutral air.

> Row after row with strict impunity
> The headstones yield their names to the element,
> The wind whirs without recollection

in a world where impunity is absolute and the idea of meaningful action ("yielding") a pathetic fallacy. The conception of nature that
had given the lives of these Confederate dead coherence and value is
gone. "Here by the sagging gate, stopped by the wall" of the ceme-
tery, the speaker feels a despair at his situation that is intensified by
his recognition of what the world buried there, and long since reduced
by time to "verdurous anonymity," had been like. (Mr. Tate particularly likes barriers that emphasize the metaphysical impenetrability
he is concerned with by their physical insignificance; the mirror of
"Last Days of Alice" is even more striking than the sagging gate of
the "Ode," in which a version of that mirror in fact also turns up in

the passage about the jaguar that "leaps/ For his own image in a jungle pool, his victim.") For Mr. Tate the cost of losing an endurable vision of nature is the loss of the world; deprived of the vision of a community and its discipline, the individual sinks into the incoherent abyss of impulse where

> You shift your sea-space blindly
> Heaving, turning like the blind crab.

This is the nightmare in which George Posey, the hero of Mr. Tate's novel, *The Fathers,* exists. "But" says the narrator of *The Fathers,* "is not civilization the agreement, slowly arrived at, to let the abyss alone?" Mr. Tate's image of the civilized man is the narrator's father, Major Buchan, whose feelings have been perfectly disciplined to the expressive social ritual of antebellum life at Pleasant Hill. There is in *The Fathers* an understanding that a civilization is subject to time and change: George Posey destroys the life of Pleasant Hill even before the Civil War destroys the social system it is a part of. But for Mr. Tate that change is simply an occasion for despair, for the recognition that we can never be Major Buchan, only George Posey.

To Mr. Warren the world of our time seems a convulsion quite as terrible as it is for Mr. Tate. But for him the world exists beyond any conception of it we may have; and it always has. We cannot know the past—but only some destructive conception of it—until we recognize that Willie Stark of *All the King's Men* is right when he says of it, "I bet things [then] were just like they are now. A lot of folks wrassling around." That knowledge about the past does not make the past meaningless, any more than the knowledge that for the same reason we will never create a Utopia makes the future meaningless. It only makes the past and future real.

In one of the several poems Mr. Warren has written about the maternal grandfather (he was a cavalry officer under Forrest) who is his Major Buchan, the grandson begins by thinking that

> life is only a story
> And death is only the glory
> Of the telling of the story,
> And the *done* and the *to-be-done*
> In that timelessness were one,
> Beyond the poor *being done*.

Then his grandfather describes how he and his men once hanged a group of bushwackers, and suddenly the boy understands that his grandfather's past life was not a story, not something that exists only as a timeless *done* but something that was once *being done* in the terrible now of time,

> Each face outraged, agape,
> Not yet believing it true—
> The hairy jaw askew,
> Tongue out, out-staring eye,
> And the spittle not yet dry
> That was uttered with the last cry.

> The horseman does not look back.
> Blank-eyed, he continues his track,
> Riding toward me there,
> Through the darkening air.

> The world is real. It is there.

But it is very tempting to deny that the life of the past took place in the real world of time, as life in the present does, and to reject the life of the present as inconceivable in the light of what one imagines the past to have been. That is what Adam Stanton in *All the King's Men* does all his life; it is what Jack Burden, the novel's narrator, does for a long time, so that when, for example, he meets the sheriff and Commissioner Dolph Pillsbury in the Mason City courthouse, he wants to believe such creatures do not exist. With repudiating irony he tells himself that Dolph Pillsbury is "just another fellow, made in God's image and wearing a white shirt with a ready-tied black bow tie and jean pants held up with web galluses." But he knows Dolph

Pillsbury is real, even if he won't admit it to himself (it is the Jack Burden who tells the story, long afterwards, who does admit it): *"They ain't real,"* I thought as I walked down the hall [of the courthouse], *narry one.* But I knew they were."

It is not that man does not need a vision of the ideal possibilities of life or that actual life does not often seem grotesquely horrible in comparison with that vision. It is not even that, for some men, it is not altogether too easy to accept the world as it is and forget its unrealized possibilities (as Willie Stark for a while does). The danger is that men who do not forget these possibilities may, like Jack Burden, refuse to understand that they are possibilities for the world and are real only in the world. The risk of trying to realize these possibilities in the world is destruction, but not to take that risk is never to live. "For if," as Shakespeare's duke says, "our virtues/ Did not go forth of us, 'twere all alike/ As if we had them not." (There are interesting similarities between *All the King's Men* and Shakespeare's "dark" comedies, *Measure for Measure* and *Troilus and Cressida.*) But it is temptingly easy, too, to think that one must not enter the grotesque reality of the world if one has any virtues.

When, in *Flood,* a prison guard refuses to shoot a madman who is murdering another guard for fear of hitting an innocent man, the Warden says, "Jesus Christ, a innocent man! There ain't no innocent man! You are fired." Yet it remains true, as the novel's cultivated lawyer says, that "When I look out the window and see some pore misguided boogers doing the best they can—according to their dim lights . . . what you might call the pathos of the mundane sort of takes the edge off my grim satisfaction." No man can afford not to shoot a murderous madman on the theory that the bystanders who are sure to be hurt are innocent (no man is) or on the theory that, since no man is innocent, men are not worth his trouble. Both theories assume that one is innocent oneself and that this innocence can be preserved by avoiding the infection of a world that is not. But the world is made up of men just like us, guilty men in ready-tied bow ties and jean pants, certainly; and made in God's image, too.

For Mr. Warren the worst is not to go into the convulsion of the world, terrible as it is to do that. No one in fact exists anywhere else. But men can deprive themselves of the responsibility (and the freedom) of being there by refusing to submit their virtues to the test of action, as Jack Burden does, or by acting as if virtue does not exist, as do the host of small-time pursuers of happiness who people Mr. Warren's novels, such as Marvin Frey, "a sporting barber with knife-edge creases in his striped pants, ointment on his thinning hair, hands like inflated rubber gloves. . . . You know how he kids the hotel chippies and tries to talk them out of something, you know how he gets in debt because of his bad hunches on the horses and bad luck with the dice, you know how he wakes up in the morning and sits on the edge of the bed with his bare feet on the cold floor and a taste like brass on the back of his tongue and experiences his nameless despair."

"Mentre che la speranza ha fior del verde," says the epigraph of *All the King's Men* (*Per lor maladizione sì non si perde/ che non possa tornar l'etterno amore,/ mentre che la speranza ha fior del verde.* By their curse none is so lost that the eternal love cannot return while hope keeps any of it green. *Purgatorio,* III, 133–135). In this Canto, Dante sees his shadow and Virgil, confessing he is lost, knows he must consult the penitents. Sinclair observes that Dante's casting a shadow "illustrate[s] the dualism of flesh and spirit . . . which is not to be resolved in theory, only in experience"; and of Virgil consulting the penitents, he says, "In this need penitence is wiser than reason, and reason is then most reasonable when it looks beyond itself. The soul's life is experience, a given thing—a *quia,* in the language of scholasticism—to be known only in living, in the last resort as unsearchable as God." (*"State contenti, umana gente, al quia,"* l.37.)

One of Mr. Warren's major objects in *All the King's Men* is to make the world of time in which experience occurs exist for us in all its ordinary, familiar, immediate reality. The novel's story of the typical political struggle in which the country boy, Willie Stark, rose to power and of his exercise of that power, of the career of Judge Irwin of Burden's Landing with its judicial integrity, its marriage for money, its deal with the power company—this story is representative of the public life of our time. It occurs in an American world that is shown in beautifully precise detail, a world of country farmhouses and county courthouses and small-town hotels, of pool halls and slum apartments and the "foul, fox-smelling lairs" of cheap rooming houses, of places at Burden's Landing and the Governor's mansion and the state capital, of country fairgrounds and city football stadiums and endless highways. Moreover, this story is told us by Jack Burden, who is (among other things) a trained historian and experienced newspaperman and can give us an authoritative account of the immediate meaning of the events, the tangled train of intentions and acts that cause them and flow from them. The world appears overwhelmingly real in *All the King's Men*. It is there. Because there is where experience, which is the life of the soul, occurs.

It is the wisdom of reason in looking beyond itself to experience that Jack Burden refuses—or is unable—to recognize until the very end, when he finally sees that if knowledge is indeed the end of man as he has always believed, "all knowledge that is worth anything is maybe paid for by blood." Until then he cannot commit his soul to experience because he cannot face what experience will do to the perfection of the story his reason has made up about life. He struggles to keep his existence a timeless preserve of images of Anne Stanton afloat on the water with her eyes closed (but even then the sky was dark greenish-purple with a coming storm) and of ideas about the world that make it unreal. "I had got hold of [a] principle out of a book when I was in college, and I had hung onto it for grim death. I owed my success in life to that principle. It had put me where I was. What you don't know won't hurt you, for it ain't real. They called that Idealism in my book I had when I was in college, and after I got hold of that principle I became an Idealist. I was a brassbound Idealist in those days. If you are an Idealist it does not matter what you do or what goes on around you because it isn't real anyway."

This Idealism was merely Jack Burden's excuse for living as if the world of time—where people try to do their best according to their dim lights and fail and grow old—were not real. He clung to this principle "for grim death" (of the soul, at least) and secretly fancied that his failure to do anything was a special kind of success. It was a way of hiding from the knowledge of experience that "was like the second when you come home late at night and see the yellow envelope of the telegram sticking out from under your door. . . . While you stand in the hall, with the envelope in your hand, you feel there's an eye on you . . . [that] sees you huddled up way inside, in the dark which is you, inside yourself, like a clammy, sad little foetus . . . that doesn't want to know what is in that envelope. It wants to lie in the dark and not know, and be warm in its not-knowing." (When Byram White's corruption is exposed he stands before Willie Stark "drawing himself into a hunch as though he wanted to assume the prenatal position and be little and warm and safe in the dark.") Jack Burden wanted to remain forever kissing Anne Stanton in the underwater world into which she took the highest dive of her life (but when they came to the surface she swam straight for the beach). He looked longingly at the May foliage of the trees and thought of himself "inside that hollow inner chamber, in the aqueous green light, inside the great globe of the tree . . . and no chance of seeing anything . . . and no sound except, way off, the faint mumble of traffic, like the ocean chewing its gums." (This lotus-eater's dream was interrupted by Sadie Burke, who told Jack Burden that Anne Stanton had become Willie Stark's mistress.)

Jack's Idealism allows him to reject as absurd caricatures of humanity the beings who fall below his standards, but it also costs him his capacity to feel, so that it is really he who does not exist humanly rather than the imperfect creatures he rejects. Anne Stanton understands this without being able to explain it.

"Oh, you just think you are sorry. Or glad. You aren't really."
"If you think you are sorry, who in hell can tell you that you

aren't?" I demanded, for I was a brass-bound Idealist then, as I
have stated, and was not about to call for a plebiscite on whether
I was sorry or not. . . ."

"Oh, Jack," she said, ". . . can't you love them a little, or forgive them, or just not think about them, or something?"

Yet he can maintain this attitude only by an effort of self-persuasion.
He has to keep telling himself that his mother is maddeningly stupid,
because he is touched by the bravery of her defiance of age and
wants to respond to her love when she smiles at him "with a sudden
and innocent happiness, like a girl"; he dwells on the ludicrous horror
of Tiny Duffy and the Boys, only to find in the end that he cannot
hate even Tiny. What is worse, he is often driven perilously close to
recognizing that what makes him think others subhuman exists in
himself. He will not touch Anne Stanton; if he does Anne will cease to
be the sleeping beauty of heartbreaking innocence he has wanted her
to remain ever since he saw her floating with her eyes closed that day.
Instead he marries Lois, who, he imagines, is merely a "beautiful,
juicy, soft, vibrant, sweet-smelling, sweet-breathed machine for pro-
voking and satisfying the appetite." But Lois "could talk, and when
something talks you sooner or later begin to listen to the sound it
makes and begin, even in the face of all the other evidence, to regard
it as a person . . . and the human element infects your innocent Eden
pleasure in the juicy, sweet-breathed machine." When Lois thus turns
out to be—honestly and stubbornly—a kind of person intolerable to
anyone of even moderate standards, Jack runs away, first into the
Great Sleep and then to divorce. Whenever Jack Burden is faced with
the dualism of flesh and spirit he runs away. His worst moment is
caused by Anne Stanton's affair with Willie Stark, when he has to
flee all the way to California and discover an entirely new principle,
the Great Twitch, to hide behind.

Just as Jack will not go into the world of experience with Anne
Stanton, so he will not give his ideas of personal conduct the reality
of action. As long as he can convince himself that he is merely a tech-
nician, he can feel he is not responsible for what is done: he is just

obeying orders. When he cannot—as when he is asked to put some real feeling into his column for the *Chronicle*—he quits. When he investigates Judge Irwin for Willie Stark, he is just exercising his technique. He had tried that once before, as a Ph.D. student, when he investigated Cass Mastern. But he laid that job aside unfinished because he wanted to keep his belief that "the world was simply an accumulation of items, odds and ends of things like broken and misused and dust-shrouded things gathered in a garret," whereas Cass Mastern had "learned that the world is all of one piece . . . that the world is like an enormous spider web and if you touch it, however lightly, at any point, the vibration ripples to the remotest perimeter." Perhaps, the narrator adds, the Jack Burden of those days "laid aside the journal of Cass Mastern not because he could not understand, but because he was afraid to understand for what might be understood there was a reproach to him."

With Judge Irwin he is again the researcher, with the research man's faith that the past is only a story, that "all times are one time, and all those dead in the past never lived before our definition gives them life, and out of the shadow their eyes implore us. That is what all us historical researchers believe. And we love truth." He does his job on Judge Irwin well: "It was a perfect research job, marred in its technical perfection by only one thing: it meant something." It had been easy to drop Cass Mastern when there arose a danger that the research job would be marred by meaning. Though Cass Mastern had lived in time, it was not Jack Burden's time and it was easy to think of Cass as part of history, "the *done*." But Judge Irwin is still alive and Jack loves him, and in digging up his past Jack has brushed the spider web. He tries not to know that, but cannot escape when his mother says, "You killed him, you killed him. . . . Your father, your father and oh! you killed him."

He has had his bad moments before, as when he caught himself defending what Willie Stark had done against the sincerely selfish businessmen at Judge Irwin's dinner party ("the bluff, burly type, with lots of money and a manly candor"). He hastened to absolve himself of responsibility ("I didn't say I felt any way," he insisted, "I just offered a proposition for the sake of argument"), but he had come very close to understanding the possibility that—as Cass Mastern puts it—"only a man like my brother Gilbert [or Willie Stark] can in the midst of evil retain enough innocence and enough strength to . . . do a little justice in terms of the great injustice." Jack Burden does not want to understand that; he wants to go on thinking that "politics is action and all action is but a flaw in the perfection of inaction, which is peace," wants to go on not knowing that his refusal to possess Anne Stanton "had almost as dire consequences as Cass Mastern's sin" with Annabelle Trice, his friend's wife, and far more dire consequences than the sin of his father, Judge Irwin, with the wife of Judge Irwin's friend Ellis Burden.

The real reason Jack Burden works for Willie Stark, just as it is the real reason Adam Stanton does, is the fascination for him of *doing* good, not just imagining it. But he does not want to recognize that to do good he must involve himself in the world where power is acquired, not without dust and heat, and what you do has all sorts of unexpected consequences for which you must take responsibility. So Jack Burden has to persuade himself that he is just Willie Stark's research man. It is not until Willie is dead and Jack discovers the part Tiny Duffy played in killing him that Jack considers acting on his own. Then he comes very close to telling Sugar Boy about Tiny. He knows that will make Sugar Boy shoot Tiny, exactly as Tiny had known that telling Adam Stanton about Anne and Willie made Adam shoot Willie.

But Jack does not tell Sugar Boy. Before he gets a chance to, he has gone to see Tiny and given himself the unearned pleasure of setting Tiny straight. Then Sadie Burke writes him that it would be foolish to expose Duffy "just because you got some high-falutin idea you are an Eagle Scout and [Anne Stanton] is Joan of Arc." That is the truth, and it makes him think of his own responsibility for Willie's death, and suddenly he feels himself caught in a

... monstrous conspiracy whose meaning I could not fathom. . . .
It was as though in the midst of the scene [with Tiny Duffy he]
had slowly and like a brother winked at me with his oyster eye
and I had known he knew the nightmare truth, which was that we
were twins bound together more intimately and disastrously than
the poor freaks of the midway who are bound by the common
stitch of flesh and gristle and the seepage of the blood. We were
bound together forever and I could never hate him without hating
myself or love myself without loving him.

That is the moment at which Jack Burden faces the truth. But until
it arrives, he is a brass-bound Idealist filled with something like despair by the insignificance of the existence he has been so careful to
persuade himself is the only reasonable one, so that when Anne Stanton says to him, "You are such a smart aleck. . . . Aren't you ever
going to grow up?" he says, "I reckon I am a smart aleck, but it is
just a way to pass the time." But it does not even do that, for he
wakes each morning to look out the window and see "that it [is] going to be another day" in the endless series of insignificant tomorrows.
Or he watches from a train window a woman empty a pan of water
and go back into her house—"To what was in the house. The floor
of the house is thin against the bare ground and the walls and roof
are thin against all of everything which is outside, but you cannot see
through the walls to the secret to which the woman has gone in. . . .
And all at once you feel like crying." For "the soul's life is experience, a given thing . . . to be known only in living. . . ." That is what
makes Willie Stark so fascinating.

Willie Stark has a gift for acting in the world. As a country boy he
had studied law and history with the passionate intensity of one who
instinctively feels that knowledge is not so much a means of understanding as an instrument of power. "Gee," he says later with amiable
contempt, "back in those days I figured those fellows knew all there
was to know and I figured I was going to get me a chunk of it." What
he knows by then is that you can use certain kinds of knowledge to
make men do what you wish, but that is quite another thing. "No,"

he says to Hugh Miller, "I'm not a lawyer. I know some law. In fact, I know a lot of law. And I made me some money out of law. But I'm not a lawyer."

He began his political career with a farm boy's naïveté by trying to get the Mason City school honestly built. When the courthouse crowd kicked him out, he ran against them on his own. But nobody listened to his story about the school and he was badly beaten. His wife, Lucy, who lives to remind him of the values power exists to serve—as Anne Stanton lives to remind Jack Burden of the power values exist to direct—reminds Willie that he did not want to be elected to a government of crooks anyway. But all Willie can remember is that the courthouse crowd had "run it over me. Like I was dirt," because they had the power. Then, with the collapse of the school's fire escape, Willie becomes a hero and it almost seems as if not mixing with crooks is the way to achieve power as well as virtue, for in no time there is the city politician, Tiny Duffy, on his doorstep asking him to run for governor. He never suspects Tiny is merely looking for a way to split the opponent's vote. "For the voice of Tiny Duffy summoning him was nothing but the echo of a certainty and a blind compulsion in him."

Willie sets out to campaign for governor with his earnest, boring, true speech, and Jack Burden and Sadie Burke watch him, full of the easy cynicism of the irresponsible wise. Yet they are reluctantly impressed by Willie. "You know," Sadie says one evening, ". . . even if he found out he was a sucker, I believe he might keep right on." "Yeah," Jack says, "making those speeches." "God," she said, "aren't they awful?" "Yeah." "But I believe he might keep right on," she said. "Yeah." "The sap," she said. When Sadie turns out to be right, they both yield to the fascination of Willie's gift for action. Sadie gives herself wholly to Willie, enduring his trivial infidelities but reacting fiercely to the real betrayal of his affair with Anne Stanton, only to discover in the end that she has helped to kill the man who, whatever he had done, she could not live without.

Willie does keep on; but not making those awful speeches. The discovery that he is once more being run over like dirt strengthens his feeling that power is all that matters, and slowly, even unconsciously, he drifts away from Lucy's understanding of the values power exists for. We watch him—as he talks to Hugh Miller, to Judge Irwin, to Adam Stanton—developing his theory that the law and the good are things men of power make up as they go along until he is—in fact if not wholly in intention—merely a virtuoso of power, half believing that by its mere exercise men can give power a purpose, as Jack Burden, his counterpart, is merely a virtuoso of speculation, half believing that by contemplating an ideal men can change the world. When Willie reaches this point, Lucy refuses to live with him anymore. But when their son, Tom, is paralyzed for life and Willie, like some pitiful Faustus, cries out that he will name his magnificent new hospital after Tom, she is there as always to remind him that "these things don't matter. Having somebody's name cut on a piece of stone. Getting it in the papers. All those things. Oh, Willie, he was my baby boy, he was our baby boy, and those things don't matter, they don't ever matter, don't you see?"

There is something in Willie that always recognizes that, too, even when he is exercising his political skill with the least regard for it. When his cunning but unscrupulous maneuver to save Byram White leads Hugh Miller to resign, he says to Miller in semi-comic woe, "You're leaving me all alone with the sons-of-bitches. Mine and the other fellow's"; and when he blackmails the legislature into voting down his impeachment, he says to Jack Burden that Lincoln seems to have been wrong when he said a house divided against itself cannot stand, since the government he presides over "is sure half slave and half son-of-a-bitch, and it is standing." When he begins to plan his great free hospital, he refuses to allow it to be built in the usual crooked way. He is not just remembering the collapse of the Mason City school's fire escape; he can prevent Gummy Larsen from building shoddily even if Gummy does take a cut of the school contract. What he is remembering is what made him want that school built honestly. This insistence that the hospital be built without graft is, as Jack

Burden says, "scarcely consistent" with Willie's constant assertions that you always have to make good out of bad, but it maddens him that Jack Burden—who has not yet learned to look beyond reason—cannot understand why, just after Willie has saved Byram White from his deserved punishment, he wants to build that hospital with clean hands.

Thus, in the confrontation of its two central characters, *All the King's Men* poses what is for Mr. Warren the central problem of existence, the irrepressible conflict between the conception of life that gives action meaning and value, and the act of living in the world in which meaning and value have to be realized. This conflict appears unendurable. Yet both Jack Burden, who tries to exist in the conception without accepting the responsibility of action, and Willie Stark, who drifts into acting effectively for its own sake, find it impossible not to know that it must be endured.

"This," as Jack says near the end of the novel, "has been the story of Willie Stark, but it is my story, too." As Willie, living the practical life of power, is haunted by a desire to use his power in a virtuous way he denies is possible, so Jack Burden, prevented from acting by his concern for the virtue he can imagine, is haunted by a desire to realize himself in the world he denies is real. This is the story the novel tells about Jack Burden. But the novel is Jack Burden's story in another sense: he tells it. It was a risk to use as narrator a central character whose changing conception of the nature of experience is the main issue in the novel. It is like making Emma Woodhouse, Lambert Strether, and Lord Jim the narrators of their novels. If it could be brought off, the meaning of the action could be revealed dramatically, from within and behind the view of a character who is limited by his own nature and does not understand that meaning for a long time; and when this meaning finally emerges on the surface of the novel, it will be the product of an experience that has been fully represented in the novel and will not be arbitrarily given, as is, for example, Marlow's view of life in Conrad's *Lord Jim*. But it is very difficult to keep separate the limited view of the events a character has

o

as he is living through them and the view he finally takes, when the events are all over and he sits down to write the story. Mr. Warren brings off this difficult maneuver, and it is well worth what it costs. But that cost is nonetheless the considerable one of making the novel very easy to misunderstand.

The voice of Jack Burden conveys three distinct feelings about the events he describes. It is, most obviously, the voice of Jack Burden the Idealist who sardonically points out the plentiful evidence that life is grotesquely absurd. He does that very effectively and what he shows us is hard to deny. At the same time the tone of his voice is almost hysterically extravagant. That extravagance gives a hectic rhetorical brilliance to his descriptions of the world's absurdities, but why should he care that much if the world is beneath contempt? His extravagance is really the expression of the second of Jack Burden's feelings, his longing to reach beyond reason to the secret of experience that he is debarred from by the refusal of Jack Burden the Idealist to believe experience is real.

The Idealist's rhetoric always belittles the world by contrasting the indignity of its shoddy physical nature with some dignified image of the soul.

> I'd be lying there in the hole in the middle of my bed where the springs had given down with the weight of wayfaring humanity, lying there on my back with my clothes on and looking up at the ceiling and watching the cigarette smoke flow up slowly and splash against the ceiling . . . like the pale uncertain spirit rising up out of your mouth on the last exhalation, the way the Egyptians figured it, to leave the horizontal tenement of clay in its ill-fitting pants and vest.

How silly to describe men in grand terms when they are all what Jack says Lois's friends are: "There was nothing particularly wrong with them. They were just the ordinary garden variety of human garbage" —whose "wayfaring" produces nothing but broken springs in cheap-hotel bedrooms, whose "pale, uncertain spirit" is only cigarette smoke, whose "tenement of clay" is dressed in ill-fitting pants and vest.

The Idealist Jack Burden is, then, always saying, "Go to, I'll no more on't." But just the same "it hath made [him] mad," or nearly so, and like Hamlet, once he is launched on a description of it, he cannot stop torturing himself ("Nay but to live/ In the rank sweat of an enseamèd bed,/ Stewed in corruption . . ."); until slowly, as we listen, we begin to feel, not that men's lives are less horrible than he says they are, but that there is some imperfectly fulfilled intention in them not unlike Jack Burden's own—some dim light—that makes them pitiful rather than disgusting. Consider, for example, Mortimer Lonzo Littlepaugh who was fired by the American Electric Power Company in order that Judge Irwin might be paid off with his job "at a salary they never paid me." Mortimer is almost as absurd as his name, and his indignation is a fantastic mixture of "confusion, weakness, piety, self-pity, small-time sharpness, vindictiveness." "I gave them my heart's blood," he writes his sister just before he commits suicide, "all these years. And they call him vice-president, too. They lied to me and they cheated me and they make him vice-president for taking a bribe. . . . I am going to join our sainted Mother and Father who were kind and good . . . and will greet me on the Other Shore, and dry every tear. . . . P.S. If they [the insurance company] know I have done what I am going to do they will not pay you." "So," as Jack Burden observes, "the poor bastard had gone to the Other Shore, where Mother and Father would dry away every tear, immediately after having instructed his sister how to defraud the insurance company"—to no purpose, he might have added, since Mortimer had borrowed practically the full value of his insurance. Mortimer Lonzo Littlepaugh was certainly grotesque, but with a passionate sincerity that is, however absurd, also pitiful.

The same double response is evoked by the tone of the narrator's voice as he describes the characteristic life of his time. "A funeral parlor at midnight is ear-splitting," he will say about a cheap joint, "compared to the effect you get in the middle of the morning in the back room of a place like Slade's. . . . You sit there and think how cozy it was last night, with the effluvium of brotherly bodies and the haw-haw of camaraderie, and you look at the floor . . . and the general impression is that you are alone with the Alone and it is His move." Or, driving past the comically tasteless and pitifully decaying Victorian houses of Mason City, he will notice "the sad valentine lace of gingerbread work around the veranda"; or he will observe the absurd and touching awe of the girl in Doc's drugstore who, seeing Willie Stark standing there at the counter, "got a look on her face as though her garter belt had busted in church." People are certainly ridiculous—vain, pretentious, foolish—as Jack Burden, who is being a smart aleck to pass the time, can see very clearly; they are also pitiful—sincere, eager, committed—as another Jack Burden cannot help feeling.

The third and most important feeling Jack Burden's voice expresses is the feeling that ultimately resolves the conflict between these two, the feeling of the Jack Burden who is telling us this story. This Jack Burden seldom speaks to us directly, and when he does it is mainly to remind us that what Jack Burden felt when he was living through these events was different from what he feels now, as he tells about them. "If I learned anything from studying history," he will say, "that was what I learned. Or, to be more exact, that was what I thought I had learned." Or he will say, "at least that is how I argued the case then"; but he does not say how he argues it now.

Only at the end of the novel do we learn that, discover that Jack Burden, without ceasing to believe in the reality of man's reason, has come to believe also in the reality of experience. Life, he now knows, is not "only a story" in the timelessness of which "the *done*" and "the *to-be-done*" are one. But if he now knows that "the *being done*" exists beyond any story man's reason invents about it, he also knows that story represents man's idea of it and determines the way he will act in it. The very existence of *All the King's Men* demonstrates that, for the controlling element in the narrator's voice is not Jack Burden the Idealist or Jack Burden the historian but the Jack Burden who has come to understand that "the soul's life is experience," and thus believes, "in my way," what Ellis Burden says as he is dying, that "the creation of evil is . . . the index of God's glory and His power. That had to be so that the creation of good might be the index of man's glory and his power. But by God's help. By His help and in His wisdom."

We sometimes hear the man who knows that in the way the narrator puzzles over an ostensibly virtuous act, as when he says of Jack Burden's conduct that night in his bedroom at Burden's Landing that Anne Stanton "trusted me, but perhaps for that moment of hesitation I did not trust myself, and looked back upon the past as something precious about to be snatched away from us and was afraid of the future. . . . Then there came the day when that image was taken from me. I learned that Anne Stanton had become the mistress of Willie Stark, that somehow by an obscure and necessary logic I had handed her over to him." Sometimes we hear it in an ostensibly accidental observation, as when he notes that "later on love vines will climb up, out of the weeds," around the sign of the skull and crossbones put up where people have died on the highway. Jack Burden does not notice that because it is relevant to his sardonic description of life in the age of the internal combustion engine; it is the image of some larger meaning of experience.

This larger meaning is in fact present behind everything he tells us, as it is behind the whole description of that drive up route 58 with which the novel begins. There is Sugar Boy taking every risk he can in order to exercise his uncanny skill as a driver and satisfy his naïve need to act effectively in the world by slipping between truck and hay wagon with split-second timing ("The b-b-b-b-bas-tud—he seen me c-c-c-c-com-ing"). There is Willie Stark enjoying every minute of this dangerous game. There is Jack Burden thinking it was a pleasure to watch if you could forget it was real, but not willing to know, as Willie Stark does, that only if it is real does it have what Cass Mastern calls "the kind of glory, however stained or obscured, [that is] in whatever man's hand does well."

That drive was a wholly natural event, the politician being driven at politician's speed to his home town to get himself photographed at

his pappy's farm for the newspapers. But it sets Jack Burden brooding about the age of the internal combustion engine and the cars
whirling along the new slab Willie had built for them, the boys imagining themselves Barney Oldfields and the girls wearing no panties
"on account of the climate" and their knees apart "for the cool." It
is an absurd way for human beings to behave; and yet Jack Burden
knows too that "the smell of gasoline and burning brake bands and
red-eye is sweeter than myrrh" and that the girls "have smooth little
faces to break your heart." It is all very like the life of man, which
moves through time at a breakneck clip that some enjoy too much
and some are too frightened by, but which is the unavoidable condition. It is far more dangerous than the gay ones suspect, for the sheer
speed of it can easily hypnotize you and "you'll come to just at the
moment when the right front wheel hooks over into the black dirt off
the slab, and you'll try to jerk her back on. . . . But you won't make
it of course." Probably not; but, as the frightened ones refuse to admit, you have to risk it if you are ever to smell the frankincense and
myrrh.

In this way the whole story of *All the King's Men* becomes a kind
of metaphor. The events of the novel are the incidents of a journey
every man takes up that highway toward the River of Death (if not
so surely to any Celestial City beyond it). For each wayfarer the
other characters represent different ideas of how to get there as in-
complete and partial as his own is for them. Each of Willie Stark's
women, for example, represents a mode of travel he adopts for a
time. Lucy, the schoolteacher, has the country people's simple notion
of virtue and lives by it with unfailing integrity, leaving Willie when
he discovers he cannot hold onto it and gain power; but Lucy has to
go right on believing that Willie, whom she had loved and married
and borne a son to, is, with all his faults, a great man. When Willie
discovers how to gain power, he takes up with Sadie Burke, who,
having fought her way up from the bitter poverty of her childhood,
plays the game of power with fierce determination; and when Willie
takes Anne Stanton as his mistress and Jack Burden, seeing Sadie's

suffering, says characteristically, "If it's all that grief, let him go," she says, "Let him go! let him go! I'll kill him first, I swear"—and does. Willie makes Anne Stanton his mistress when he discovers in himself a need not just for power but to do good with clean hands. Anne Stanton has shared something of her brother Adam's dream of an ideal past in which those who governed were heroic figures; she has always known it is not enough, but it makes her able to give those who, like Willie, govern now a sense of greatness. Anne comes to love Willie when she learns that he, whom she had supposed a wholly wicked man because he was not perfectly good, has done much good—"Does he mean that, Jack? Really?"—and that her father, whom she had supposed perfectly good, had done evil. Each of these women is for Willie Stark the embodiment of the idea he lives by while he loves her, as Willie is for each of them. So each character is for all the others he knows.

Through most of the novel, Jack Burden is suspended between Adam Stanton, the friend of his youth, and Willie Stark, the friend of his maturity, and between Ellis Burden, the father who had loved to make the child Jack Burden happy and lived only to care for the helpless children of the world after he learned that his wife had become the mistress of his best friend, and Judge Irwin, the father who did not scare but loved Jack's mother and took her, was an upright judge all his life except once, when he was desperate, and taught Jack to shoot ("You got to lead a duck, son").

For Jack, Adam Stanton is the romantic who "has a picture of the world in his head, and when the world doesn't conform in any respect to that picture, he wants to throw the world away. Even if it means throwing out the baby with the bath. Which . . . it always does mean." Jack ought to know; it is what he did when he refused to touch Anne Stanton. Adam Stanton refuses to believe people need anything but justice. But Willie Stark, who, like Judge Irwin, has the courage to act what he feels, is one of the people and knows that "your need is my justice." Jack Burden is, to start with, too like Adam Stanton to believe that the grotesque world he lives in can be put together again, even by all the king's men, and for a long time he refuses to touch it. But in the end he is too much like Willie Stark not to understand Willie's dying words—"It might have been all different, Jack. You got to believe that"—and to know he must try. As the novel ends, he has married Anne Stanton and is living with her in Judge Irwin's house, that relatively permanent—and lifeless—expression of the values handed down to him from the past, writing the history of Willie Stark's life. But he and Anne are about to leave that house and the writing of history and to enter the process of history, the life of their times. "And soon now," as Jack says in the novel's last sentence, "we shall go out of the house and go into the convulsion of the world, out of history into history and the awful responsibility of Time."

Index

About the Author

Arthur Mizener has been a professor of English at Cornell University for fifteen years. Born in Erie, Pennsylvania, in 1907, he attended the Hill School and graduated from Princeton University in 1930. He received his M.A. from Harvard University and his Ph.D. from Princeton. He taught at a number of places, including Yale University and Carleton College, before going to Cornell. Since then he has been a Fulbright lecturer at the University of London and has held Guggenheim and National Endowment fellowships. He is the author of a biography of F. Scott Fitzgerald, *The Far Side of Paradise,* and a number of other books concerned with Fitzgerald's work. In 1963 he published a collection of essays called *The Sense of Life in the Modern Novel,* and he is now at work on a biography of Ford Madox Ford.

Arthur Mizener is a professor of English at Cornell University. He is especially well-known for his biography of Scott Fitzgerald, *The Far Side of Paradise*. He is now at work on a biography of Ford Madox Ford.